D0146583

The Entrepreneur's Guide to Writing Business Plans and Proposals

The Entrepreneur's Guide

CJ Rhoads, Series Editor

The Entrepreneur's Guide to Writing Business Plans and Proposals

K. Dennis Chambers

PRAEGER

Westport, Connecticut
London

Library of Congress Cataloging-in-Publication Data

Chambers, K. Dennis, 1943–
 The entrepreneur's guide to writing business plans and proposals / K. Dennis Chambers.
  p. cm.—(The entrepreneur's guide, ISSN 1939–2478)
 Includes bibliographical references and index.
 ISBN-13: 978–0–275–99498–3 (alk. paper)
 1. New business enterprises—Planning. 2. Business planning. 3. Proposal writing in business. 4. Business writing. I. Title.
 HD62.5.C423 2008
 658.4′012—dc22   2007035294

British Library Cataloguing in Publication Data is available.

Library of Congress Catalog Card Number: 2007035294
ISBN-13: 978–0–275–99498–3
ISSN: 1939–2478

First published in 2008

Praeger Publishers, 88 Post Road West, Westport, CT 06881
An imprint of Greenwood Publishing Group, Inc.
www.praeger.com

Printed in the United States of America

The paper used in this book complies with the Permanent Paper Standard issued by the National Information Standards Organization (Z39.48–1984).

10 9 8 7 6 5 4 3 2 1

This book is dedicated to
Elijah, JC, and Tess

Contents

Acknowledgments

Hundreds of people have contributed knowingly or unknowingly to my development as a writer. So many others have generously given of their time and advice for this book that it is impossible to name them all.

Gerry Young, Grant Chambers, Kenneth Peters—submariners all!

Len D'Innocenzo, Jack Cullen, Kristie Janes, Philip Madell, Dr. Linda Coleman, John Connorton, Peter Raisbeck, Steve Delchamps, Erica Neal, John Fredette, Paula Chambers, Nora and Peter Waystack, Mike Irwin, Bradford Moses, Don Hudson, Brian Harwood, Don Balducci, Dr. Stephanie Hancox, Paul Faulkner, and Don Koonce all contributed directly in some fashion, with my thanks. I'm also grateful to the friendly and professional staff of the Newburyport Public Library, and to the thousands of participants and students in my writing workshops and college classes.

And to Jeff Olson, editor extraordinaire, without whom . . .

Introduction

Business writing is a one-way street.

This bedrock truth separates business writing from all other kinds of writing. And understanding it separates the winners from the losers. For example, I am sitting here at my laptop thinking about you. Who are you? Why are you reading this? Can I help you with your specific challenges? However, in this writer/reader situation, I'll likely never know the answers to these questions about you because you'll never tell me. Our communication is a one-way street: me to you. This book will succeed, then, only if I can correctly imagine who you are and what you need in order to write better plans and proposals.

Chances are you are a business professional—an entrepreneur—experienced enough to be good at what you do and young enough to see a long road of many wins and some losses ahead of you. That is the picture I have of you in my mind, anyway, and it will serve as a foundation for writing this book. All the other myriad, complicated, interesting aspects of your life and personality are irrelevant to me because I'll never know them. My educated guesses about you will have to serve. Fortunately, I have met in my business career many people like you—people who are smart, educated, ambitious, and eager to be successful. I have turned their faces (in my mind) into a collage of images that I call The Reader. This is the kind of thing that business writers do all the time, and I believe it is necessary in order to hit the mark.

Another dark secret of business writing is that we normally get only one shot at our target. Whether your target is a venture capitalist or a bank loan officer, a marketing director or a company president, you'll be lucky to have one run at that person. If you fail, it's over.

This notion of talking with an unseen, unheard, unresponsive audience is unique to business writers. Stand-up comedians have an audience sitting right there in front of them, and they can adjust their delivery, pace, and content as the audience dictates with their responses. Movie producers use test audiences to fine-tune a film before releasing it into the great unknown. (If the film is unsalvageable, there's always direct-to-video.)

Artists have color and canvas. Composers have music and players of instruments. Pilots have ground control. Tightrope walkers have nets. Novelists can bring a successful character back again and again for another shot at immortality.

But business writers have none of those things. We sit at our keyboards in a cone of silence, praying for inspiration, trying to conjure up that elusive Reader and hoping that we're right. Even such greats as Charles Dickens and Arthur Conan Doyle had the luxury of writing serial chapters for monthly magazines; they adjusted the plots according to the reactions of readers. When Sir Arthur, weary of his cocaine-addicted detective, sent Sherlock Holmes tumbling over the Reichenbach Falls, there was such an outcry in the land that he was forced to bring him back from the dead for a few dozen more stories. But you and I are not writing detective stories or movie scripts. We are business writers trying to inspire particular action in our readers, and that requires writing specifically to a person.

Soon, you'll have to do the same thing—picturing in your mind a client, or prospect, or even suspect about whom you know little. You'll make some educated guesses, of course. If there's time and if it's appropriate you'll do some research about the persons and organizations you are trying to influence. The more you know about them the more finely you can hone your presentation to win the account or receive the action you desire.

A novelist or playwright, on the other hand, has none of these concerns. He is trying to write literature that creates pleasure or drives contemplation, not action, and so writes not for you, the reader, but for himself—the artist. There are exceptions, of course. William Shakespeare, to name one, wrote for money. He didn't bother to concoct his own plots, but simply took them from others and turned those plots into plays of soaring power. He wrote "The Merry Wives of Windsor" on direct orders from the queen—for money. In many ways, Shakespeare was as much a business professional as he was a poet. (Now aren't you sorry you slept through *Hamlet* in high school?)

But he was a notable exception. Most writers of literature write on the side, for pleasure, after working at their day jobs. The myth of the starving full-time writer is often not far from the truth.

Nowhere is applying these principles more important than when it comes to the challenges of writing business plans and proposals that bring us profit today. The way we used to write them yesterday is over. That way no longer works. Think of the premier maker of buggy whips on the day Mr. Ford rolled out his first production car. On that day, buggy whips were no longer useful. Mass television advertising, to cite one example, is essentially over as a medium to market to large numbers of prospects. Selling door to door is essentially over. Telemarketing is in its last days.

I'm facing the same challenge right now. Do people still read books? Evidently you do, so that makes two of us. You can buy software that will ask you some foundational questions and then write your business plan for you. But is that what you want? I think not, because no book filled with model plans or plan-writing software can ever know you and your business and your prospects as well as you do. That's why no computer program or pre-written model can give you the one thing you need to know in order to succeed—the secret to writing powerful, customer-centered plans that get results.

In this book I will give you some good models, of course. But more importantly, I'll give you the techniques for focusing on your readers and prospects that you're not likely to find in any other source.

So you and I, business writers, are writing for specific reasons having to do with the reader. We are, for example, answering a customer complaint, or persuading a venture capital firm that we are a good risk, or proposing that a company send its marketing budget in our direction. We are writing for readers who have names and job titles and babysitter problems and insecurities about their 401(k)s. We are going to the effort of writing, not for their pleasure, but to get some sort of action out of them. Our aim is to motivate them to do something.

Therefore, our task is *all about the reader*.

As I write this, there is a crane operating on the street just beyond my window. On the long arm of the crane, in large letters, is this: "Height 4 Rent."

Ah, now there's a smooth operator. He knows that if ever I'm in the market for a tall crane I'm buying one thing: height. My aim would be to get up high. (Personally, I get vertigo on a thick rug, so I'm not actually a potential customer, but you know what I mean.) On that crane arm he doesn't write "The #1 crane company in New England" or "The latest Framitz 890 hp engine." No. I'm not buying either of those things. I'm looking for height. So he tells me that's what he's selling. Perfect.

By contrast, on the bank just up the street is a sign in the window: "Serving this community for 128 years." Do I care about that? Not even a little. They lose.

I have spent considerable time as a professional writing instructor. At the beginning of every class or workshop, I hit this point hard. It's not about you; it's about the reader. You and I will succeed or fail in our writing to the degree that we persuade or fail to persuade readers that all the contents of our document are for their benefit.

One example: Recently I was hired to consult with a large financial management company regarding their outreach materials for new business. They were losing more pitches than they were winning and were wondering why.

I asked them to give their new-business presentation to me, an audience of one.

The PowerPoint show started out with a photograph of "the four founders" taken in the 1940s. I stopped the presenter right there. "Are any of these men alive?" I asked. "Yes," was the reply. "One."

"Is that person involved in the business today?" I asked.

"No," was the reply.

Next slide: a close-up of Founder "Smith." Next slide: Founder Smith in his office circa 1955 tapping on one of those hand-crank calculators.

I stopped the show again. "Are you going to give me a biography of each of the founders, most of whom are dead?" I asked.

"Yes," was the reply.

"Coffee break," I said.

In our twenty-first century, no one is interested in your founders, at least not at the beginning of a business relationship. People care about themselves and their challenges to compete in a savage marketplace. If you can help them with what they care about, they will stick around for a few more minutes. If you clearly care about yourself and your business more than you care about them, they will leave.

Now if you actually stayed awake during *Hamlet* you're probably thinking of the line: "There needs no Ghost, my lord, come from the grave to tell us this" (Act I, Scene 5). I agree; it seems *obvious* that our primary concern should be our readers. Well, after years of reading business documents that are all about the writer, I believe that we all need to be reminded of the obvious every day.

Just think of me as your friendly ghost writer.

I

HOW TO WRITE
A BUSINESS PLAN

1

Start from Strength: What's in It for Me?

If you can't outplay 'em, outwork 'em.

Ben Hogan, professional golfer

This is a good place to start. If you don't see the benefit in writing a killer business plan, you might not do it, or you might do it poorly. So let's look at some of the reasons for writing an effective plan.

I am taking the time to write an effective business plan because:
(please check all that apply)

— My financial institution requires it.
— Writing something down makes it real.
— I want to impress potential investors.
— I want to get working capital.
— I want others to see my Big Idea.
— Others have recommended that I do it.
— I want to think on paper.

All of these reasons (and many more) are worthy. You may even have checked most of them. I think you need an effective business plan because you need to do this kind of thinking before you start spending too much money.

THE VALUE OF PLANNING

General Eisenhower said "In preparing for battle, I have often found that plans are useless, but planning is indispensable."

The general was suggesting that there is power in the process of writing down a plan, even though plans change. I emphasize the writing aspect of a plan here because ideas have life only when they are written down. If the plan exists in your head only, or in bullet points on a few cocktail napkins, it is not written down. It is a prayer or a wish, but it is not a plan. Writing clarifies thinking. We write plans down to clarify them for ourselves and all other interested parties.

While we are in the rarified company of flag officers, here's another from a man who ought to know: "A good plan executed right now is far preferable to a perfect plan executed next week" (General George S. Patton, Jr).

Plans change. But that is no reason to resist writing one. For example, if you were writing the first business plan for UPS back in 1907, you would write something to the effect that the company is specializing in messenger service in cities.

If you were to write a new business plan for UPS in the 1960s, you would observe that the package handlers are working from sheets of plywood placed on wooden sawhorses in buildings that were formerly gas stations.

Today's UPS has a sorting facility in Louisville that is one of the largest buildings on planet Earth, with miles of conveyor belts delivering computer-controlled packages directly to waiting airplanes. Today's UPS repairs laptops, shapes baseball bats, stocks parts for Bentleys, provides warehouse storage for shoes and cameras, and refurbishes cell phones. Oh, and they also deliver packages worldwide.

That is an example of stunning growth and an evolving business mission over a century. But it didn't stop them from writing a good business plan for its time in 1907.

Fred Smith wrote a now-famous business plan for Federal Express in business school for which he even more famously earned a gentlemanly "C" from the professor. That business plan has little relationship to today's FedEx, but we wouldn't have today's FedEx without that first business plan.

Similarly, nothing should stop you from writing a good plan now. Tomorrow will happen whether you have a plan or not. So let's have one.

TIME FOR A NEW DISCUSSION ABOUT BUSINESS WRITING

This book emphasizes the *writing* of plans and proposals. Of the dozen or so books available on business plans, none deals exclusively with how to write them using twenty-first century sensibilities except this one. That being so, you and I must make important assumptions:

- You have a product or service for which there is demand in the marketplace.
- You have clearly defined your customer base.
- You know how to reach your customers.
- You are one of the best professionals on earth to provide this product or service. (If you hate baking, don't try to sell cookies.)
- You understand what investors look for, from hard-nosed venture capitalists to your soft-nosed friends and family.
- You understand at least the rudiments of balance sheet accounting and have good software to help you do it.

What makes this the time for a new look at business writing is the reality of our lives in this new century.

First, free nations and free enterprise are devoting much of their wealth to increased security. Monies that perhaps would have been available for new commercial ventures ten years ago are often used to enhance the safety of people and organizations. This is not bad news, of course, if you are running a start-up whose mission is to enhance security across a wide spectrum of concerns, from airport screening to Web impregnability. Nevertheless, against this broad canvas of challenges, business is tougher and investment capital is tighter and competition is fiercer than at any time in my personal memory.

This means, among many other things, that if you are trying to build business by using writing, you face a formidable challenge.

Second, the fundamental nature of finding customers and selling to them has changed. And if that's true, as I believe it is, it means your writing must reflect these new realities and use that awareness to make things happen.

Case in point: On October 30, 2006, newspapers across the country reported that the Yale School of Management is reinventing itself. I found the story in the *Boston Globe*. According to Joel M. Podolny, the new dean, the school has decided to drop traditional B-School courses such as marketing and finance in favor of an interdisciplinary model that will account for the new challenges that twenty-first century business leaders will face. Courses on economics and organizational behavior will be supplanted by such courses as "State & Society," "Competitors," and "Sourcing & Managing Funds."

What are some of the important new business realities of the twenty-first century? Compare your list with mine, or add to it.

1. The foundations of our economy are different since the turn of the new century. They feel tender, even fragile. We are now more connected, for better or worse, to everything important that happens in the world. A few years ago, chaos theory suggested that a butterfly flapping its wings in Chile could result in a tornado in Topeka. Now we have seen that even a hint of trouble in one part of the world could affect energy prices or stock market anxieties in another part.

2. Our readers are different in this new century. They all grew up with television as a constant presence in their lives. Many of them think MTV, for example, is too slow-paced for their taste. (MTV, hovering at the thirty-year mark as I write, makes nothing of this milestone, lest viewers be reminded that the network is older than they are.)

3. Our readers have different expectations. The days when readers were willing to sit through pages of point and counterpoint are over. Many of today's middle and top executives are video gamers. Not former gamers—current gamers. They are used to failing and starting over. They like noise and action. And they want everything that happens to be fast.

4. Our customers are different. We can't find them as easily as we used to. They are watching network television less than they did ten years ago. They don't read any particular magazine or listen to radio stations that have commercials the way they used to. They are biking down

mountain trails or working on a new interactive game or tasting the new balsamics from Sicily. They are not sitting around waiting for us to sell them something.

5. The media are different. Newspapers are fading in importance. Ask anyone under thirty how long it has been since he read a newspaper cover to cover. Network evening news now appeals to people who need denture creams and the latest wonder drugs (ask your doctor). Today's young execs get their news from shows such as "The Daily Show" and from standup comics. You can find news online faster than radio or television can deliver it to you. Recently, I printed out a $5 coupon for the parking garage at the airport. The coupon is available only online. Without the Web, that parking enterprise would have neither means nor budget to reach me. When was the last time you watched a TV commercial without lunging for the remote? Digital recording systems make broadcast programming schedules obsolete. Bottom line: We can't reach customers the way we used to, and yet with some of the new changes we can reach customers who were heretofore unknown to us. Web access is as common as electric outlets and the Internet is a vital part of our lives. E-mail and Instant Messaging have changed how we all communicate, and along the way have deeply influenced the language.

   The speed of our media transformation was brought home to me recently when I asked my college writing students to bring in a piece of music that they particularly admire and come up with three arguments why we should all like it as well. I dutifully and without thinking toted in my semi-portable CD player to the class, along with a fine recording by Thelonious Monk. The students all looked at me in the blank way that only college students can achieve. None of them had CDs; they all had those little handheld computers about the size of a chocolate bar that can store 100,000 songs. Duh.

6. The future is not what it used to be, as Yogi Berra said. Amen, brother. If your boss matriculated into the executive ranks during the 1980s or 1990s, she is now facing a future that few business professionals ever envisioned. China is a behemoth capitalist country that pretends to be communist. Americans are taking back service jobs from India and Pakistan because the cost savings simply weren't worth the loss of customer satisfaction. Sourdoughs are back mining silver in Nevada because the price of silver now exceeds the cost of processing ore. We're squeezing oil from shale in Canada for the same reason. The future is ever-changing and ever-elusive. Nothing is predictable anymore. People who use the phrase "for the foreseeable future" are kidding themselves. What will happen when you can no longer count on tomorrow being somewhat similar to today?

7. The things we have to know to survive are different. It has been said of John Stuart Mill, who died in 1873, that he was the last human being on earth who embodied all the knowledge of his time. His father brought him up to acquire all knowledge, which he did with a vengeance. However, J. S. Mill, if he had to take the entrance exam to

get into MIT today, would likely fail miserably. There is so much to know now that no one person can possibly absorb even a large portion of it. Your readers are probably in the habit of acquiring the knowledge they need to succeed in their industry—a pursuit that involves most of one's waking hours. They don't have time for any extraneous prose from anyone else.

In this context, our writing must evolve along with all the other aspects of global business. It has to be leaner, faster, and utterly reader-focused. Anything less will be ignored.

PLANNING TO WRITE: DO YOUR RESEARCH

Now that we've taken a quick look at some of the environmental changes that impact any business, let's look at you and your plan for your business in the same light. What can we say about you in the plan that potential investors will find compelling? Who are you? This question looks simple on its face, but is quite complex.

Consider my friend "Jack." I've known him for decades, ever since we served together as young officers on a Navy ship. He is a good, loyal friend. He's a husband and father. He's a raconteur of the first rank. He is highly educated and brilliant in his chosen field, corporate law. He is a senior partner in a prestigious Wall Street law firm. He is a squash player and an arts patron. He is at times a power walker, a political power broker, and a museum goer. And, oh yes, an honorary Commander of the British Empire, as certified by her majestic self Queen Elizabeth II.

So ... who is he really? To me, simply a friend. To his clients, an advocate. To the Queen, an honorary subject. He is all these, and many more. While Jack is complex, he is not unusually so. You are just as complex as he is.

If a business plan is a kind of resume—an application for investment capital and future success—you can't put everything important about you in the plan. What do you put in? What do you leave out? The answer changes with every plan writer, but the means to discover the answer is always the same: It depends on the reader. What is the reader looking for? How can you find out? Or failing that, how can you make your best guess?

Scenario One: You Can Ask the Reader

This is not as far-fetched as one might think. You are going to a good deal of trouble and expense to write and publish a business plan. So why not ask some of your potential readers exactly what they are looking for? The worst thing that can happen is that you'll end up in voice-mail limbo. The second-worst thing is that they will tell you to put it in writing and don't bother them. Well, okay, you were going to put it in writing anyway. I recommend that you make a few phone calls to a few prospective readers, ask if you might interview them, and listen carefully to what they tell you.

Here is an excellent structure for that interview:

- Facts
- Issues
- Needs
- Dreams

This F-I-N-D interview system was invented by Len D'Innocenzo and Jack Cullen, two of the leading trainers of sales representatives in the United States. The F-I-N-D system provides a strong framework that will lead you to some remarkable insights if you follow it closely.

If you study the framework for a moment, you can perceive its inherent strength. It begins cold (just like you would in a telephone call or in-person interview) and moves quickly into warmth. It is focused entirely on the subject, not on the questioner. And it leads to an evolving sense of trust. People will not reveal their thoughts or their true selves to someone they do not trust. And above all else you want the interviewee to trust you. Let's look at each step in detail.

Facts

First, begin with facts. The other person doesn't need to trust you at all to discuss facts, so it should be an easy conversation. Some facts you might ask about:

- What kind of businesses do you prefer to invest in?
- Are you the person to whom I should address my plan?
- Do you have any experience with businesses in my industry?
- What time frame is typical from receiving a plan to deciding whether to invest in it?
- What is your company's attitude about the market for personal care products?
- And so on.

Issues

Next, move into the area of issues. Issues are the broad, general trends and concerns that people talk about at industry conventions. Answering these requires some level of trust from the interviewee, but not much. For example:

- I've read that venture capitalists are moving away from high tech for the next year or two. Is that your understanding as well?
- What are the investor trends regarding personal care products?
- Do you have any experience yourself with investing in a product whose marketplace is mature?
- And so on.

Needs

Third, talk about needs. Needs are far more intimate than issues. People talk about needs around their own conference tables, not at industry conventions.

- After researching the field, I would like to have your firm invest in our company because I agree with your stated mission. Do you see any possibility for a match here?
- Are you trying to balance your portfolio with non–high-tech enterprises?
- Are you potentially interested in companies whose market reach is North America only?
- And so on.

Dreams

Finally, there is the area of dreams. Dreams are personal. We reveal our dreams to few people, if any at all. In most cases, D'Innocenzo and Cullen recommend asking the dream question—if at all—only in person, only one to one, and only at the end of an interview. Responding to the dream question requires a high level of trust from the person you are interviewing. It means you have established your professionalism with the other person. If there is any chance at all that the person will not answer it, then don't ask it. Most people are comfortable asking "dream" questions on the professional level: "If our plan is well received and your firm invests successfully in us, what would that mean to you professionally?"

A personal dream question might go like this: "Matthew, if we were to go through your process successfully and be added to your investment portfolio, what would this mean to you personally?"

"Their response to the dream question means a great deal to you," says Len D'Innocenzo. "It means you have established trust. It means they are likely to go forward if you meet all their other criteria. And it means your interview has been successful. Of course, you never reveal their answer to anyone. But it gives you a level of trust that your competitors may never achieve."

Most people never ask the dream question. But some of those who do tell me it provides them with insights they would never otherwise have.

Scenario Two: You Cannot Ask the Reader

If you cannot, under any circumstances, speak directly with decision-makers, then you will have to give your company its sharpest delineation. You will have to make your company come alive to a person who is simply sitting at her desk and reading about it. The only way to do this successfully is with powerful truth, and that comes only from a world-class mission statement. Because a mission statement is not about you—it's about the image you wish to have in the minds of your customers.

YOUR MISSION STATEMENT: THE FOUNDATION ON WHICH YOU BUILD YOUR COMPANY

Let's turn now to the foundation of any successful business plan: the mission statement.

Defining the Business Mission

The focus of a business plan is to define the organization's mission for the enlightenment of all concerned, from venture capitalists to staff members to bank loan officers to temporary interns. With it, you are trying to demonstrate to everyone that you will be successful in two vital areas by providing:

1. An analysis of the benefits that current and potential customers seek and that you provide.
2. An analysis of existing and future environments that you and your competition will create.

Further, a good mission statement provides for your three most fundamental needs. First, it arouses interest in the investment community. Next, it gives managers and staff a core of identity that helps them understand the work they are doing and their own place within those day-to-day functions. Finally, it provides a platform for advancing into the future.

Here's a good working definition of a mission statement:

Mission Statement: A brief but motivating prose description of the organization's purpose for being. It should be short enough to memorize and long enough to inspire and inform any person who wishes to know why the organization exists and whom it serves.

Stephen Covey, in his book *First Things First*, warns that mission statements are often written by senior executives and ignored by line workers. Worse, I have found in my consulting with scores of companies that line staffers frequently make fun of the mission statement, creating their own parodies that would leave the original writers aghast. That's why it's vital that your mission statement be organic—understood and believed by everyone who draws a paycheck from the company.

A mission statement is, in effect, the organization's unique genetic identity. It establishes *who we really are* for the rest of the world.

The firm's long-term vision, embodied in the mission statement, establishes boundaries for all subsequent decisions, objectives, and strategies. It should focus on the markets you expect to serve, not on your executives or your products or services.

I think a useful mission statement needs to be six important things:

1. *True.* I have worked for companies whose mission statement said they wanted to be the best this or the finest that. They tossed in words like

"excellence" and "world-class" but those were just words. They didn't mean it because they didn't do what it takes to really be excellent and world-class. Preparation is all, whether you want to paint a house or win a football game or become a successful enterprise.

2. *Easily Memorized.* "The Lord's Prayer" is useful to millions of people because they can memorize it. When I was in elementary school we said "The Pledge of Allegiance" because it was short and memorable and helped to remind us who we were. What you remember, you own. You want everyone who works in your company to know the mission statement word for word. If they own it, they will do it.

   If you are tempted to make your mission statement longer than three or four paragraphs, consider the U.S. Air Force. Chances are, your organization is not as big as the Air Force, yet here is their entire mission statement as of this writing: "To deliver sovereign options for the defense of the United States of America and its global interests—to fly and fight in Air, Space, and Cyberspace."

   Even I could memorize that.

3. *Inspiring.* Every U.S. Marine, before becoming a corporal or a gunnery sergeant or a colonel, before learning how to fix vehicles in the motor pool or cook stew in the mess hall or trace coordinates on a map, is a rifleman. Every Marine knows the Rifleman's Creed. It begins this way: "This is my rifle. There are many like it, but this one is mine. It is my life. I must master it as I must master my life."

   Your mission statement is the way to master the life of your company; it's good when everyone embraces it.

4. *Defining.* Dr. Martin Luther King, Jr., provided the mission statement for the civil rights movement in his "I have a dream" speech in Washington, D.C. He said the movement is for those who want human beings to be judged not by the color of their skin but by the "content of their character." It was a defining moment for the world. A good mission statement lets everyone outside of the organization know where you stand and helps them determine where they stand relative to your enterprise.

5. *Exclusive.* A good statement separates your group from all others. Is Burger King fundamentally different from McDonald's? Of course it is. Is one dental practice different from another? Like night and day. Why would you choose to buy a cookie from Mrs. Fields rather than from Famous Amos? They are different entities. Your mission statement helps prospects decide whether you are the right choice for them. And also whether they are right for you.

6. *Regularly Recited.* Think of some organizations that have been around for a long time: The Catholic Church. The Marine Corps. United Auto Workers. The Boy Scouts. General Motors. Procter & Gamble. Crest toothpaste. One thing they have in common is a regular habit of reminding themselves who they are and what they stand for and why they do what they do. Some long-standing organizations are faltering and in danger of collapsing because they have forgotten who they really are.

SOME MISSION STATEMENT EXAMPLES

Here are some famous mission statements:

- Mary Kay Cosmetics: "To give unlimited opportunity to women."
- 3M: "To solve unsolved problems innovatively."
- Wal-Mart: "To give ordinary folk the chance to buy the same thing as rich people."

These have the benefit of being short and memorable. Here's a classic statement from the National Oceanic and Atmospheric Administration's National Weather Service: "Working together to save lives."

Mission statements don't get much better than those five words. So if I work there, should I come in on a Sunday afternoon if there is a tornado threat in Oklahoma? Yes, if it saves lives. Should I agree to help the Coast Guard with a weather prediction for Georges Bank fishermen tonight? Yes, we work together. It's beautiful. The agency statement goes on, as government statements tend to do, but even then it's good stuff:

The National Weather Service (NWS) provides weather, hydrologic, and climate forecasts and warnings for the United States, its territories, adjacent waters and ocean areas, for the protection of life and property and the enhancement of the national economy. NWS data and products form a national information database and infrastructure which can be used by other governmental agencies, the private sector, the public, and the global community.

LensCrafters for years has had an informal mission statement that they use in their marketing and advertising communications: "We help the world to see better." I think that is brilliant. I asked LensCrafters to share their full mission statement with me, and they sent me about 190 words on their eyewear and manufacturing expertise and distribution network. What all those words are really saying is: We help the world to see better. Every product they sell, every employee they hire, every commercial they broadcast is built on that vision of themselves. They distribute glasses free to people in need around the world because such activism fits with this mission statement.

Calloway Golf has been a technological leader in golf equipment for two generations. Their memorable mission statement: "Every product should be Demonstrably Superior and Pleasingly Different."

Nike's genetic code is breathtakingly precise: "Authentic athletic performance." Every activity of everyone who works for Nike derives from that basic understanding of who they are. They will not hire an employee, or cast a spokesperson, or buy a company that does not also participate in authentic athleticism. Nike does not spend a nickel trying to sell products to me because I am not an authentic athlete. I'm a weekend warrior with the sore tendons to prove it. I might buy a Nike product or two along the way, but they do not waste money going after me. They spend all of their marketing dollars on real athletes. When you have that kind of focus, many of your decisions are easy.

And when employees know about, agree with, and participate in your mission statement, life gets easier still. I believe that the most successful organizations nurture that sense of mission in everyone who works there. When it becomes a mantra, it becomes real.

I was teaching a series of workshops for administrators in one of New York's leading hospitals. I was impressed with the unity of the group regarding their corporate mission. "What makes you different from all the other hospitals around here?" I asked.

"Our mission," a woman named Miranda said.

"And what's that?" I said.

"Well," she answered, "our president sums it up for us every day. The main thing is to keep the main thing the main thing."

"Wow," I said. "That's your mission statement? I love it. And what is the main thing?"

The entire group responded as one: "Customer service."

"So," I said, pretending to be Socrates, "you are in your office laboring over a financial report due by day's end, and an elderly gentleman walks by, looking confused. Do you help him or not?"

A person who actually worked in accounting said, "I would get up from my desk and go ask him if he needed help."

"Let's say," I said, "that he was looking for the x-ray department. What would you do?"

"Take him there," several people said at once. They wouldn't give him a map or write down directions. They would take him. They said it was not possible for a customer to get in the way. The reason they are there is the customers. I promised to call each of them if ever I needed medical help.

"You'll like us," Miranda said with a smile. I believed her.

Studying mission statements is like eating potato chips—hard to stop. Here's one of my favorites from the U.S. Secret Service website:

The United States Secret Service is mandated by statute and executive order to carry out two significant missions: *protection* and criminal *investigations*. The Secret Service protects the President and Vice President, their families, heads of state, and other designated individuals; investigates threats against these protectees; protects the White House, Vice President's Residence, Foreign Missions, and other buildings within Washington, D.C.; and plans and implements security designs for designated National Special Security Events. The Secret Service also investigates violations of laws relating to counterfeiting of obligations and securities of the United States; financial crimes that include, but are not limited to, access device fraud, financial institution fraud, identity theft, computer fraud; and computer-based attacks on our nation's financial, banking, and telecommunications infrastructure.

The power of a good mission statement is incalculable. It may mean the difference between success and failure. And the boss should write it. A mission statement written by a committee looks like a mission statement written by a committee.

I also like short mission statements: one or two or three sentences. That forces you to focus and get down to bedrock quickly. Following are some guiding thoughts that might help you to write it.

CREATING A GOOD MISSION STATEMENT AND SITUATIONAL ANALYSIS

To create a mission statement, ask yourself the following questions:

1. What is our unique genetic identity? Who are we, in other words, deep in our bones?
2. List five qualities that separate us from all other competitors.
3. If we have been in business for over a year, how would our customers define us? (Don't guess on this one. Ask them.)
4. If we were to launch a national advertising campaign, who might be an appropriate spokesperson for us? Why?
5. Who are our customers precisely? ("Female aged 18 to 49" is not precise.)
6. What human need does our product or service provide for?
7. Name three of our toughest competitors.
8. How is our marketing landscape likely to change in the next five years?

If you write down these questions and your answers, you will be far along the path to a widely useful mission statement. Please write down your thoughts and save them. "Writing," says well-known literary theorist Walter Ong, "is a way of organizing the mind."

The one successful company that I know of that doesn't seem to have a mission statement (they may have one; I just couldn't find it) is Les Schwab Tires. With four hundred stores throughout the western United States they don't talk the talk—they walk the walk. Or rather, they run the run. They might not need a mission statement because they embody it every day. (They do talk about goals. Their literature contains this: "Our company goals are to continue to provide the legendary Les Schwab level of customer service, to be original and innovative, and to stay independent.")

Talk about a commodity—a tire is a tire is a tire. Or so one would think. You can buy tires anywhere, from the corner gas station to Sam's Club. So why go to Les Schwab?

If you've ever done business with them, you know that when you drive up to a Les Schwab tire center, someone in a clean uniform will run to your car. Yep, run. They don't walk, skip, or strut. They run! You can be sure that within a few seconds of your arrival, someone will run to greet you. Now there's a mission statement! I don't need to see it in writing, when I can see it in running.

The Value of a Situation Analysis

You might also find it useful, after creating your mission statement, to conduct a classic situation analysis. It is a way for you and your readers to understand the current and potential environment in which you will be selling your product or service.

Textbooks refer to a situation analysis as a SWOT analysis: a way to identify your company's internal Strengths and Weaknesses and to examine your external Opportunities and Threats.

It is good to write your SWOT analysis boldly and clearly. For example:

Strengths

- Low personnel turnover.
- Clear and inspirational mission statement.
- Clear need in the marketplace.
- Wide-ranging experience of top executives.

Weaknesses

- New CEO with limited industry experience.
- Poorly defined product image.
- Top operations people are nearing retirement.
- Aging machinery.

Opportunities

- New CAD/CAM software offers manufacturing efficiencies.
- May merge with a French engineering company.
- Level two competitor has been bought by a conglomerate, leaving some customers adrift.
- Relocating operations to a plant in the Midwest will reduce expenses by 23 percent.

Threats

- Downward trend in core customer incomes.
- Entire industry is "mature."
- New, more efficient technology is in development.
- New competitors from China and Brazil are encroaching on our markets.

From there, while still in the brainstorming stage with your group, you might like to begin formulating your professional marketing mix: a blend of strategies for distributing, promoting, and pricing your product or service. But I'll leave the planning to you—after all, you know your industry, and your strengths, better than anyone.

MODEL PLAN FOR A SMALL, HOME-OFFICE BUSINESS

Let's wrap up this introductory chapter with a good model plan for a small business. It contains elements we haven't discussed yet, but never fear: We'll cover them all in the next few chapters.

As with most of the model documents in this book, they are true to the original work of the authors, but I have made up the names. If I use the names or initials of real people and real companies, it is coincidental.

This is the business plan of a professional in major-retail communications who launched a venture of her own several years ago. She has seen steady growth with the addition of one or two new clients a year. She used this plan to borrow nearly $15,000 from a local bank to invest in equipment and modest marketing materials. She has since paid off the debt and is a recognized force in her niche market.

NMI BUSINESS PLAN: EXECUTIVE SUMMARY

Introduction

New Marketing Innovators (NMI) provides Marketing Communications and Public Relations support to clients including corporations, small businesses, nonprofit organizations, marketing/advertising agencies, and independent print and web designers.

Founded in 2003 by sole proprietor Kerri Parker, NMI has achieved consistent sales growth as well as a solid reputation among clients, colleagues, and industry professionals with whom NMI subcontracts projects. Subcontracted individuals comprise NMI's "virtual team" of "innovators," including print and web designers, copywriters, printing companies, and any other support personnel with whom NMI collaborates or outsources project work on an as-needed basis.

Opportunity

To compete in today's fast-paced marketplace, virtually every business or organization must communicate and promote its services to various audiences—internal (employees) and external (prospects, clients, colleagues, affiliates, etc.).

The appropriateness and application of marketing communication types, styles, targets and distribution methods often vary based upon the organization's category, brand strategy and unique goals. What remains constant, however, is the need throughout every organization for clear, concise, and consistent marketing communications.

Three major types of prospects represent opportunities for NMI to be of service:

1. *Small business owners.* Owners either have marketing ideas but no time or expertise to implement OR owners do not have ideas and need someone to plan and implement marketing activities.

2. *Business development managers in corporations.* These professionals need the support of a dedicated marketing professional to assist them in achieving their goals. Often they are capable of doing the work themselves, but either do not have the time or resources.
3. *Other professionals in the creative or communications field,* such as print and web design professionals, copywriters, print and broadcast media advertising representatives, and more.

Business Concept

Drawing upon eleven years of marketing and management experience with a Fortune 100 company, NMI principal Kerri Parker assists clients by identifying and developing cost-effective methods to enhance and communicate their image in accordance with their schedule and budget.

Industry Overview

Several types of similar and complementary professionals also serve all or a portion of the needs of NMI prospects. Competition includes full-service advertising agencies; other independent contractors or marketing-related consultants who have similar career experience; and/or others with a similar business model as NMI.

Target Market

See above, in Opportunity section: Three major types of NMI prospects.

Competitive Advantage

Kerri Parker's experience, energy, and core competencies of skilled project management and concise, results-driven business writing are the vital elements she provides in helping clients achieve their marketing and public relations goals. In addition, Kerri has assembled a team of highly skilled, creative, results-oriented and competitively priced professional subcontractors with whom she regularly completes projects.

The advantage for clients is ACCESS to reliable, local, affordable SINGLE-SOURCE support for essentially all of their marketing communications and public relations needs.

Management

NMI principal Kerri Parker is the sole and final decision-maker regarding company management.

Support personnel includes the Parker family CPA and Financial Planner, each of whom is familiar with the business and upon whom Kerri sometimes relies for advice (mostly financial or tax related).

Financial Highlights

Cash flow/accounting. NMI has no outstanding long-term debt. All income and expenses are managed using QuickBooks software. Typically, NMI clients are invoiced on a monthly basis, with payment terms of net 30. Most clients use NMI on an as-needed basis, and some clients have a retainer agreement in which they pay a set monthly fee for ongoing NMI services.

Expenses. Subcontractor and professional service provider expenses; office supplies and equipment; communications expenses (phone(s), fax, and Internet); regular dues to professional associations and networking groups; media subscriptions to print publications including newspapers and business/trade magazines.

Income sources. Retainer clients, project-basis clients; and markup on subcontracted services.

Status

NMI has achieved consistent annual sales growth since the company was founded in 2003.

Goals include:

- Introducing more "project-based pricing" versus hourly rate pricing, but this is often difficult or impossible to implement, owing to the constantly changing nature of client needs.
- "Productizing" services in order to package and sell them on a consistent basis, with initial heavy involvement (creation of content) and eventual minimal involvement (re-use of a system or service once the learning curve or set up is complete).
- Assisting clients with being more proactive versus reactive. This requires educating the client on the value of planning, and the use of disciplined and strategic approaches to help clients plan strategies that will better serve them in the long term.
- Shift client base to include a greater amount of medium or large companies (with greater dedicated marketing budgets), as opposed to primarily small companies or independent professionals who require constant education, justification, and reassurance regarding value and investment for marketing.

This is a modest plan, appropriate for a home-office enterprise that Kerri had already started with her own savings. Please notice several strengths of this document.

1. It is well written. Kerri uses all the tools of professional writers to pull readers in and keep them reading. Here are some of those tools; I'll go into more detail about them later.

- *Short Sentences and Short Paragraphs.* I recommend your sentences be no longer than fifteen words and your paragraphs no longer than five typed lines. This enhances reading. Some writers I know like to write long sentences and multi-page paragraphs simply to demonstrate erudition. Well, most of us are not selling erudition. We are selling a product or service. We are trying to get the attention of readers who know nothing or little about us. And we are trying to demonstrate the strength of our ideas. All of that happens with short, crisp writing.
- *Subheads.* She uses subheads as topic labels—fine in a short piece. I like to see hard-working subheads that take readers in a clear direction. I give you examples of such subheads all through this book. Subheads are like signposts that guide readers in the right direction. I think they are vital for success in writing today.
- *Plain English.* Simple, direct words are the best choice for business readers. Don't try to dazzle them with vocabulary. Dazzle them with ideas.
- *Active Voice.* In reading thousands of business documents, I have seen the great majority of writers use passive voice as their default choice. Here are some real-world examples of passive voice used unnecessarily:

  - "Floors should be washed at the end of every shift."
  - "Time sheets should be submitted before close of work on Fridays."
  - "Mistakes were discovered in processing your account."

  Active voice puts the person or thing doing the action in front of the verb. As in these examples:

  - "The accounting department waives the need for a signature for any expense under twenty-five dollars."
  - "Jennifer sent the documents to you by interoffice mail yesterday."

  If you have any confusion about active versus passive voice, please go to the section on grammar for the twenty-first century and do some of the exercises I have provided.

2. It is specific. Under "Opportunity," for example, Kerri lists the three kinds of professionals who are the core of her target market. The more specific your plan is, the better your readers can picture it coming true.
3. It focuses on the future with a positive attitude. Not enough has been written about the advantages a positive attitude—about everything, all the time—will give you, especially in writing plans and proposals. Positivity shines through and helps put the reader on your side. People like sunshine.

Now, on to more about capturing the interest of your reader—the one possibly in a position, remember, to help your venture along, or stop it in its tracks.

Capture the Elusive Readers: What's in It for Them?

My Three Secrets of Success:
Get up early.
Work hard.
Find oil.

J. Paul Getty

Reminder: I am assuming that your business plan, like the great majority of business plans, is going to a disinterested reader whom you have never met. If you are sending your plan to your friendly local banker, with whom you play golf on Saturdays, you have a different challenge. If your written plan is to help you obtain startup money from family and friends or "angel" investors, that's a different challenge also. For now, let's go for the biggest quarry of all: a professional investor such as a decision-maker in a venture capital (VC) firm whom you do not know. Further, you are sending your plan to several VC firms, as well as other potential investors, so it is not possible to write the entire plan for one specific reader. A customized cover letter for each reader—yes. But the forty-page plan itself will be difficult to customize if you have several dozen readers.

Nevertheless, create a reader in your mind and make certain guesses about this person. Here are some to start with:

- She is a professional with solid experience in business and finance.
- She will receive perhaps as many as 750 business plans each year.
- Her average reading schedule is somewhere between three and four plans a day.
- She doesn't read plans every day, preferring to spend a good portion of her time in the field or doing research.
- Her boss expects her to bring in about one entrepreneur a month for an in-person presentation.

These are guesses, true enough, but they are useful ones. And we are already starting to create a two-dimensional mental image of our reader. We can make some further assumptions, based on our own research and experience.

Let's start with packaging. Why? Because it is the first impression the reader receives from you, in most cases.

She will discard perhaps 10 percent of submissions without reading even the first page because they are inappropriately packaged. A good business plan tends to come in around forty typed pages, and is single-spaced, with one-inch margins, flush left and ragged right, serif typeface (such as Times Roman), and includes well-conceived graphics. It tends to be spiral bound or inside a half-inch three-ring binder or some other professional covering— the kind any good office supply store can provide for you. If the plan is perfect-bound (like a paperback book) and handsomely printed, she will worry that you will spend too much of her investment money on sizzle rather than steak, on fine leather chairs around a teak conference table, rather than on sales and marketing tools.

So our idealized investor has already reduced her reading load by seventy-five before she even reads the executive summary. Total left for the year: 675.

Please note: I think 10 percent is far too low, but I'm trying to be conservative. I suspect the real figure for amateurish submissions is around 25 percent. Most investors are tight-lipped about this point, not wishing to admit that they relegate a large portion of plans to the round file.

By the way, if you send a document to a person who has not requested (or agreed) to read it, then that person is under no obligation to read it or even to handle it carefully. It's always a good idea to get the reader's permission before sending a document.

Now she picks up a business plan that is inexpensively spiral bound but neat and carefully prepared. She hefts it. Heavy. She checks the number of pages: 139. She puts it aside for another day when her schedule is lighter. That wonderful day may or may not arrive this year. She picks up another one and it almost flies out of her hand. Nineteen pages. Too light. Perhaps the writer hasn't prepared sufficiently. She'll get to it later, possibly.

Let's say 15 percent of the remaining submissions are too heavy or too light. She has not tossed them, but it will be a long while before she gets to them: 574 plans to go.

She picks up the top one from this reduced pile and begins reading. The name of her firm is misspelled. There are two typing errors on the first page of text. She casually flips through a dozen or so pages and picks up a typo or grammar error on each one. Into the rejection pile it goes. If she's a typical investment reader, 10 to 20 percent of submissions contain these inexcusable errors and she will discard them. In her mind, poor grammar is a symptom of sloppy thinking. This may be unfair, but it is how the world works. Without having read so much as a page yet, she has only 488 plans to go.

And yours is one of them.

You have given yourself a shot—it's still a long shot—but at least it's a chance. She's looking for only fifteen or twenty good plans, remember, making your odds around 24:1. Even the tightest casino on the Las Vegas strip will give you better odds than that. So let's consider how your plan can make it to that final group of twenty.

Diving into the Money Pool

Here's a rundown of the people in a position to invest in your company:

Venture Capitalists. I'm using VC professionals as an example of the toughest, most jaded readers you will have. Sell your idea to these people, and you can sell to anyone. The important thing to remember about them is that they are not philanthropists. They won't lend you money because they like you or because you make a spectacular pitch to them. They lend money when they are convinced that your financials are sound and they will get their investment back with interest. And the money they lend often comes attached with large strings that look to some entrepreneurs like anchor chains. They might demand a piece of your business, or a say in your top management team. They might contract with you only if you agree to sell the business when it reaches a certain level of profitability. And so on.

Local Banker. Your friendly local banker, on the other hand, may have philanthropy in mind when he decides to lend you money. Perhaps he likes the positive impact your business will have on the neighborhood, or the local economy. Perhaps he went to college with your father and attended your christening. Whatever. He is still looking for solid financials, but he has other concerns and other loyalties that affect his decision. He will likely read everything you write in your plan. Your banker will be glad to advise you about a standard commercial loan or a commercial line of credit.

SBA. Another excellent source for working capital is, of course, the Small Business Administration (SBA). Their hard-working website (www.sba.gov) is a rich resource for new entrepreneurs and small to medium startups. Their congressional charter is to help small businesses with their financial problems and they are highly motivated. Their website also contains dozens of well-written (if brief) sample business plans.

Friends and Family. Even people who like and trust you expect you to shuffle the cards before you deal. They also expect a well-written business plan because it is simply good business. You have many other resources for working capital, from equity in your house to credit cards; any good accountant can advise you about all of your options. (If she recommends credit cards, find a new accountant.) I have included a wide-ranging chapter on financing issues written by an expert. You will likely find the answers to most of your questions there. Financing is, after the overarching vision of your enterprise, the greatest concern to all potential investors. If your financials are solid and embedded in hard-working prose, you have given yourself the best possible chance for success.

TURNING AROUND OUR POINT OF VIEW

Let's approach our challenge of writing a business plan from the only perspective that really counts: the reader's. For a few minutes, take the part of a disinterested reader who is for the first time looking at your well-written, appropriately packaged business plan. What immediate questions are going through his mind? I shall list a few, and suggest that if you answer them wisely you will have your plan already started. Please feel free to add your own questions, and answer them as well.

Workbook Questions: What My Reader Wants to Know

1. What is the essential nature of this business? A sophisticated reader is looking for the *real* answer here, not the obvious one. Let's say you have decided to open an advertising agency that specializes in Web marketing. Not for you the classic venues of television and radio broadcasts, or newspaper and magazine print layouts. You are helping clients market themselves in the Web space. So the obvious answer is: "I create opportunities on the Web for clients to put their brands in front of actual prospects in memorable ways, thus reducing marketing cycles for clients and increasing revenue opportunities for my company."

   Okay, good. But have we reached bedrock? Maybe the following would do it:

   "The Web environment is constantly changing faster than any medium in history. Only those professionals whose single medium of expertise is the Web have any chance of keeping up with the changes, and on rare occasions initiating the change. My company offers the unique opportunity of success to clients who understand that the Internet is built on interaction—and who are willing to use that interactivity for profit."

   Is that closer? Perhaps. It is more specific, and perhaps more enticing for an investor to get a glimmer of what will make your enterprise succeed.

   Another good way to think of your business is to consider its genetic makeup—its DNA, if you will—that gorgeous double-helix shape that's the foundation of all identity. Your double helix is the reason you are unique in the universe. There has been no one like you, and never will be again. Similarly, every branded business is unique. The brand known as King Arthur flour, for example, is genetically different from Gold Medal flour. The chemical composition of the two flours might be similar, possibly even the same, but the brand identities are nothing alike.

   King Arthur flour, may I suggest, is for serious bakers, the kind who labor over a flaky crust and swoon when the filling is contained within the confines of the pie. King Arthur flour is produced in Vermont, a state with a long and enviable history for producing quality foodstuffs. Many food-related companies relocate to Vermont simply to get that highly desired "Made in Vermont" label. And with their bakers' catalogs, cookbooks, and related baking products, King Arthur strives for a close, old-fashioned relationship with all of their customers.

Gold Medal flour, by contrast, is a behemoth division of General Mills, assumed by most people to be based somewhere in the vast Midwest. Betty Crocker, one of the greatest American marketing icons, is their spokeswoman, although no one has actually ever met Ms. Crocker. (To be fair, I've never had a chat with King Arthur, either.) What determines which of these flours I buy is a function of the mood I'm in, and not the siren songs of the flour makers. Notice that I, as a potential customer, get to say what the particular brand image is, at least in the kingdom of my own mind. The same will be true for your customers, no matter how hard you try to be clear about what your brand image is. The two images—the one in the consumer's head and the one the company promotes—are likely to be similar, if not identical. But the wise marketer understands that the *customer* ultimately decides what the real brand image is.

Gold Medal mass-produces flour arguably as fine and useful as King Arthur's. If I wish to assembly-line a few hundred pancakes for the next breakfast fundraiser at the local Rotary club, odds are I'll stock up on Gold Medal. It is certain to be fresh and reliable. If, however, I'm devoting a rainy Saturday morning to perfecting a pumpkin scones recipe for brunch with our best friends, I'll turn to King Arthur. Why? I'm not sure. But it just feels better to bake something special with flour from a Vermont manufacturer while rain is dripping off the eaves and Mozart is riffing on the stereo. Further, one could also point out that I am simply following the brand identity that each company has been at pains to create over many years. For you and me, there is no such thing as a commodity. Every brand is unique. The winners understand fully that uniqueness.

Remember New Coke? I grieve to bring up painful memories, but the example is so illustrative of the power of customers to determine brand identity.

A generation ago, Coca-Cola thought *they* owned the brand. Research told them that consumers liked the new formula they had spent years testing and developing. They launched the new flavor with great fanfare. And there was a hue and cry in the land that no major brand had ever heard before. Around the globe, lovers of caramel-flavored sugar water wanted *their* old Coke back. Sure, thousands of tests had convinced the company that people liked the new flavor. But Coke neglected to ask the only important question: Would you be willing to switch to the new Coke? Turns out, we were decidedly not willing.

How was it possible for the most recognized brand name in the world to make such a colossal error? Well, it was easy. Coke thought they produced and we accepted—end of story. The moral of the tale is clear, even for a much smaller brand like yours. Create the best product or service you can. Build the brand as well as you can and create a matrix of loyal and somewhat loyal customers. Then follow where they lead you. Listen to them. Do what they want. This is the interactive twenty-first century, after all.

So. Whether you are just starting your company, or looking to expand an established business: who are you really?

It is critical to know the true answer to that question. Because if you're not sure, your competitors will be eager to provide the answer for you.

These questions aim directly at your enterprise's genetic uniqueness. Please think about them, and put your answers in writing for later reference. Your answers will form the basis of your plan.

- What is the single most important reason why my customers will come to me rather than to my competition?
- If my competition can provide a similar product or service at a cheaper price, will my customers prefer coming to me anyway? Why?
- Is the nature of my business likely to change in the next five years? If so, why? If not, am I asking for trouble?
- Is the nature of my corporate genetics inflexible? If yes, then how precisely sure am I that customers don't want me to change? (This question is difficult on its face. Ivory Snow, for instance, has been 99 and 44/100 percent pure since the nineteenth-century. The formula has not changed since your great-grandmother was a child. The Ivory soap you buy at the mega-mart is the same Ivory soap she bought at the general store. Now consider Gillette. They have been the leading brand in men's shaving equipment for a century, and are not likely to give it up anytime soon, even with recent changes in corporate structure. Their early advertising theme is a clue to their DNA—if you want to look sharp and feel sharp, use Gillette. Of course the company's products have changed over the decades. Their double-edged "safety" razor was the standard for thirty years, and a rite of passage for acne-challenged teenage boys on their way to the sock hop. Those two edges gave way to two parallel blades and now they're up to three and our grandchildren may be shaving with ten blades at once for all I know. But if you asked any man who uses a Gillette razor— and that's most men in America—why he uses it, his answer will likely have something to do with looking and feeling sharp. Just like the blades themselves. So the marketing tactics change, but the DNA is unchanged. That's why defining your corporate gene structure is vital.)
- If a better, faster, or cheaper way to do what I do comes along, will I be able to respond well enough to stay in business? (If, for example, your business is providing custom brochures to small businesses in your area, will you be able to compete with a business that offers semi-custom brochures at half your price?)
- In one or two sentences, what is the genetic foundation of my business concept?

2. Who are my best customers and prospects? Any investor will look carefully at who will buy your product or service. You need to have this nailed down.
3. What does a snapshot of my finances look like now? What will a snapshot look like two years from now? Five years from now?

4. What do I want this business to become? Do I want to stay small and customer-focused? Do I want to get big and become a manager of others?
5. Why am I taking such a risk, knowing that most new businesses fail in the first two years?
6. Finally, what do I want the reader of my business plan to do? This question may seem obvious, but is worth exploring. What do you want her to do? The first reader at any large VC firm will not give you approval for investment capital on the spot. The best you can hope for is that she will move you on to stage two, whatever that means in her firm. Realistically, if she likes your plan she will probably put it into her "Second Look" pile and keep reading through her original stack. If she is really impressed with your plan, she may call or write to you to come in for an interview. Whatever the next step is, you have no control over it. But you do have control over your plan's power to step out from the pack.

Having a solid grasp of what your business is really about, and of where you want to take it for the next five years, you are ready to start writing the plan itself.

So let's take a look at an abbreviated structure for our plan. We are particularly interested in the optimum flow of topics that would interest *this* reader. For our purposes I have created a company out of thin air—it bears no relation to any similar company anywhere in the world. I will not attempt to write the entire plan at this point. It would have little relevance to your plan anyway. We are going for the impact of ideas communicated in a fresh writing style to persuade the reader.

With an image of our idealized reader firmly in mind, what is the optimum order of the topics that she will care about?

The Traditional Method of Organizing a Business Plan

You may prefer to organize your plan in the traditional way recognized and recommended by many business schools. Here is one such typical organization:

1. Customized Cover Letter.
2. Table of Contents.
3. Executive Summary.
4. Background.
5. The Company.
6. The Market.
7. Competition.
8. Personnel.
9. Sales and Promotion.
10. The Financials.
11. Appendix.

NEW CHALLENGES REQUIRE NEW THINKING
AND NEW WRITING STYLES

The essential elements of an effective business plan have been fixed by long tradition, and they are listed in the sidebar. The order of the elements, however, and the way you deal with them in prose, deserve a fresh look. As I noted earlier, this is a new era for entrepreneurs. The ready availability of awe-inspiring computer power makes it possible for any dreamer with a laptop to compete with you. The Internet, combined with flawless overnight delivery service, means your true competitors can now be several countries—not just several counties—away. Businesses that were once limited by data storage capacity, for example, now find unlimited storage and retrieval online or in micro servers for a fraction of the cost a decade ago. Many manufacturers now have virtual pipelines in place with cheap-labor countries for fast design and delivery of goods at costs far cheaper than even a few years ago. Anybody can compete with anybody.

Then there is the question of time. We're out of it. American business is now on a hyper-speed schedule that is going in only one direction—faster. Ad agencies are putting commercials online in a matter of hours, not weeks, and adjusting offers and pitches on the spot in response to consumer feedback. Marketers can get top-line results within minutes after their research is concluded. Publishers are delivering whole books to readers on personal electronic devices days before the printed versions hit bookstores. Profits now depend on speed more than any other single factor.

"Oh brave new world, that has such people in it," says Miranda in Shakespeare's *The Tempest*. She is right, and you are one of those people. The way you write your business plan has to reflect that newness as well.

Here is one way to construct, sequence, and write your business plan that reflects today's realities. I'll mention the elements here, and expand on them in the next chapter.

1. *Customized Cover Letter.* Gives a full range of contact information. Most importantly, it highlights for the reader the single best-selling idea. It showcases the organization's energy and desire to achieve its vision. And it tells the reader what you want the reader to do. If your aim is to be invited in for a presentation, say so.
2. *Table of Contents.* For any document over ten pages.
3. *Executive Summary.* A synopsis of the entire report in two or three pages. Emphasizes the genetic uniqueness of your company and suggests the nature of the matrix in which your enterprise will operate.
4. *The Financials.* Investment-oriented readers will focus on how you will capitalize and maintain your company near-term and long-term, so give them the full financial picture early in the plan. This is a checkup of your financial health.
5. *The Company.* A full description of what your company will look like under real-world operating conditions, and complete personality profiles of the principal officers.

6. *The Landscape.* A discussion of the larger industry in which your business is located. What are the clear trends? What is the shifting nature of the plate tectonics on which your industry is founded?

7. *The Market.* Now and in the near future, a discussion of who will buy your products or services, the market's growth potential, and any possible restrictions that will negatively affect your market.

8. *The Competition.* A full discussion of who your competitors are and their relative strengths and weaknesses compared to your company's.

9. *Personnel.* Who will carry out the mission of your company, and where will they come from? Are you oriented toward outside sales representatives? Is it an in-bound telephone order operation? What is the function of your staff relative to sales and profits?

10. *Sales and Promotion.* How will you reach the best prospects for your products or services? Are there any natural restrictions on where your prospects can come from? A beauty salon, for example, has an obvious geographic limit on how far its customers are willing to travel.

11. *Appendix.* This is a repository of everything that could possibly help your capital-generating goals, from graphs and maps to marketing surveys and even transcripts of conversations.

This is the basic structure. Wise entrepreneurs will add any other elements that they deem important. For example, if you are planning to open a company that makes and bottles pasta sauce, you will need to provide a discussion of the various state and federal regulations that apply, as well as a description of your plant. If you intend to provide same-day package delivery service to a certain geographical area, you'll want to discuss renting versus owning the vehicles, maintenance plans, insurance, and so on.

So let's tackle these elements one at a time in the next chapter.

3

Conquer the First Draft:
The Easy Part

> Just take the ball and throw it where you want to. Throw strikes.
> Home plate don't move.
>
> > Satchel Paige, Hall of Fame pitcher

Theories abound about writing the first draft.

Many nonprofessional writers are daunted by the challenge, seeing it as the hardest work of all, laboring over the details and continually checking for spelling and punctuation errors, as well as more-felicitous phrasing. Over many years I have encouraged business writers to see writing the first draft as the easiest part of the entire process.

The hardest part is preparing to write.

Ben Hogan, one of golf's all-time greats, said often that whether he won or lost a tournament was predetermined by the kind of preparation he did before the tournament and not his play during the match. His success on the field was a function of his preparation. If you are looking to win new business, you might adopt Mr. Hogan's philosophy for your own.

Here's an analogy that might help when it comes to writing.

If you have ever painted your living room in a fresh coat of color, or put new stain on tired old clapboards, chances are you have modeled the way professional writers go about their craft.

What's the hardest part about painting? Is it brushing on that bright new coat—the first draft, if you will? No. For most of us, the hardest part of any painting job is the preparation. I spent several weeks last summer refinishing ten exterior window sills on my newly purchased 200-year-old house. Installed when Paul Revere was still alive, the thick, antique blocks of wood were now parched and seamed with cracks and crevasses. The paint that the previous owner applied was chipped and bunched and weary after a dozen harsh New England winters. With the wood so delicate and dry, I had to remove the old paint carefully with fresh stripper and a small blade without doing more damage. Next I had to fill the cracks with wood filler, let them dry for several days, then sand and vacuum the dust and reapply and re-sand and re-vacuum. All this was hand work that took several weekends to do properly.

At last, the day arrived when I was ready to put on the first coat of oil-based marine primer—expensive stuff made for the long haul. I was all set to enjoy the work on a lovely summer day.

It took an hour.

The next day, the second coat took another hour. The day after that, the finish coat took about fifty minutes.

The paint job took me three weeks to prepare, three hours to paint, and another three or four hours to clean up.

The percentages for a writing job are about the same as for a painting job.

Preparation: 50 percent
First draft: 20 percent
Clean up: 30 percent

Another helpful way to think of writing first drafts has to do with the "left-brain/right-brain" theory of how the mind works. First set forth by Dr. Roger Sperry in the 1960s, the theory has gained traction by people studying the elements of human creativity.

You've heard of the model. Our brains are divided evenly into two hemispheres. The right side of the brain controls the left side of our bodies; the left side controls actions on the right side of our bodies. This much is for certain. Dr. Sperry added some valuable psychological insights on what had been considered to be a purely physical phenomenon. He suggested that the right side of our brains controls human emotional qualities such as fear, creativity, imagination, and so on. The left side, he said, is our logical functions such as mathematics and linear reasoning.

Contemporary thinkers have added greater richness to the theory.

Industrial societies such as our own, they say, emphasize the left-brain, cognitive activities that are required for success: analyzing details, following text instruction, and understanding sequence, to list a few. Modern life requires a fully developed left brain.

Right-brain thinking, by contrast, lives for simultaneity. It specializes not in text but in context; not in sequence but in the big picture. Right-brain thinking is not so valued these days, but ironically it's what got us here alive.

Picture Moog, one of our early cave-dwelling ancestors. It's night. The firelight does not extend to the mouth of the cave. Suddenly there's a noise, and he sees a shape with horns coming into the cave out of the darkness. There's no time for sequence or rational deduction. Does he strike out in defense, run, or simply stay where he is? That determination is a function of the right brain—a much faster processor, it turns out, than the left brain. (Some researchers suggest twenty-five times faster.) Our long-ago ancestor decides instantly, taking in all the sensory input available, that it is only Oog, coming home from a successful hunt with a deer on his shoulder. So Moog does not strike out at Oog, and there's venison with remoulade sauce for dinner tonight.

The right brain, in other words, holds the real power.

You write your first draft with the right brain.

My advice is simple. Write the first draft as fast as you can, in a warm or hot frame of mind. Write without correcting, without going back and revising, without correcting spelling or grammar or punctuation. Write write write, just the way most professional writers do. That's using the full power of your right (synthesizing) brain.

Once the first draft is written, go back and revise in a cool or cold frame of mind. Editing is a left-brain (sequencing) function that does its best after the right brain is finished working.

If you try to write a first draft using both hemispheres of your brain, you'll find yourself writing-deleting, writing-deleting, writing-deleting. That way leads to madness. Use one hemisphere at a time in proper order, and life is easy.

Still not sure about the power of the right brain to keep you alive? Imagine this: You're driving down a country road at night, late in the fall. Unbeknownst to you, the outside temperature has just dropped below freezing. Driving into a slight turn you feel the wheels slide on new ice and the car begins to drift out of control. Whatever actions you take at that moment will be dictated by your instantaneous right brain. There's no time for the left brain and its sequential processing. You need all the input *now* to avoid disaster—and that's your right hemisphere's job. When it comes to writing the first draft, your right brain is your best friend.

Let's create a startup company so I can model for you how to go about writing the various elements in a good business plan. The company is small- to mid-sized, a manufacturing enterprise with mail-order customers potentially around the world. Its only product, thus far, is Nurse's Choice, the healing crème for hard-working hands.

I won't write the full plan. For one thing, of the hundreds of business plan models available to you in books and online, you'll be able to find many that are similar to the plan you have in mind to write. For another, your company is likely to be quite different from my model, so my particular prose won't be that much help to you. I mainly want to suggest how you can think through your writing task and make it as appealing to a disinterested reader as possible.

THE CUSTOMIZED COVER LETTER

I recommend you write the cover letter last, just before you package your plan for delivery. That way you'll have the entire plan in your mind and can underscore its best benefits for the reader.

You have three objectives:

- Get the reader interested in the plan and your enterprise.
- Stress the uniqueness of your product or service.
- Suggest next steps.

Here is one good way to do it.

September 19, 20XX

Ms. Janice Cunningham
AdVenture Investments
146 Main Street
Midtown, OH 12345

Subject: A startup company with a ready-made, worldwide market

Dear Ms. Cunningham:
How do your hands feel right now?
Most of the people I talk to tell me their hands feel tired, dry, chapped, weary, or stiff nearly all the time at work. Air conditioning dries our skin. Frequent hand washing is vital for continued health, yet it also makes hands feel raw and chapped. Life, in other words, is hard on everyone's hands.
Will you take a moment to try the small sample of hand crème I enclosed along with this package?
We call it "Nurse's Choice: the healing crème for hard-working hands." After 18 months of product testing, this hand crème is now ready for a worldwide launch and I'm hoping it will intrigue you enough to discuss investing in its success with me.
If you have just now applied it to your hands you'll see that it is soothing and non-greasy. In a few minutes, the aloe and apricot mixture will make your hands feel soft and smooth—and younger. The fresh citrus aroma will give your nose a treat. It is this combination of aroma and texture that people say makes this the most pleasant and efficacious hand cream they have ever tried.

Developed by an RN, Nurse's Choice Wins All Clinical Tests

Leigh Nielsen, a Registered Nurse and avid herbalist, developed this cream for her own use. When some of her hospital colleagues tried it, they became instant converts and insisted she make some batches for them to buy. In a profession where people wash their hands five to seven times an hour, this was high praise indeed. Almost overnight, the entire hospital staff was using it, including surgeons and maintenance people.

Now Nurse's Choice Is Ready for Market

My partners and I have taken this product as far as we can with our own resources. In every clinical test it is a winner. We are seeking investment capital to rent and equip a moderate manufacturing facility to produce and begin marketing Nurse's Choice to the U.S. market using radio and Internet advertising, website retailing such as eBay, and (to begin) a ten-person sales force.

Next Step

Ms. Cunningham, if Nurse's Choice (along with our plan to be profitable within 24 months) appeals to you, we would welcome a chance to come in and present our plan to you and your colleagues. Your website stipulates that you do not wish to receive phone calls from entrepreneurs, and of course we will honor your wish. You are one of only six venture capital firms we are contacting. We will wait to hear back from you. Thank you for your time. My business card is enclosed.

Sincerely,
Joseph K. Altsheller
Address and contact information

Why This Model Cover Letter Works

First, it is friendly and approachable in tone. There is no gonzo vocabulary, no absurd superlatives, no purple prose. It is in plain English and easy to follow.

Second, it uses subheads to guide the reader. Subheads are one of the great secrets of professional copywriters, and the basic working tool of all direct-response writers. The fact that professional writers use subheads universally should tell you something about the power of subheads to guide and persuade.

Third, it uses mostly short sentences (no more than fifteen words) and short paragraphs (no more than five typed lines) to be easily understood.

Fourth, it uses active voice throughout.

Fifth, it is positive. There's not a negative notion anywhere.

Sixth, it respectfully suggests next steps.

Seventh, it is mostly about the reader, with enough new-product discussion to whet the appetite.

An Additional Note about Subheads

Subheads are valuable for a variety of reasons. They act as signposts, telling readers what's ahead and enabling them to skip a paragraph or two if they wish.

They tell your whole story in just a few words, which are then amplified in the paragraphs that follow.

They keep the reader on track with your thinking, helping both reader and writer to focus on what is important. Subheads have influence; they set the reader up to see things your way.

Finally, they suggest professionalism and power.

That's why I recommend you use subheads liberally in all of your business documents. Some general subheads that serve a wide variety of uses include:

- Next Steps
- What This Means for You
- Actions Requested
- Why This Matters

A True Story about Using Subheads in Business Writing

Several years ago I was invited to teach a full-day business writing workshop to twenty-five senior executives of one of the world's largest office-equipment manufacturers. It was a gratifying session with lots of interaction. When we got to the part in my presentation about using subheads, I pitched it hard.

But the group was having none of it. A white-haired presidential-looking gent explained to me that his was a worldwide, conservative organization, a hard-headed enterprise that could not use any device as "slick as the kind of subheads that advertising people use, no offense." The others, smelling blood, piled on. "That's right, J.B. No subheads for us!" "What else ya got, Dennis?"

I was losing the argument until one of the younger execs, "Frank," raised his hand and asked for calm. "Wait a minute," he said. "This makes sense to me, and I'll tell you why."

He proceeded to tell the group about an experience he had the day before. Recently hired, Frank was early for a meeting with his boss, who was in the inner office with the door closed. So Frank sat in the anteroom where the administrative assistant worked, a woman named Bonnie. While Frank was waiting, the mailroom guy delivered a stack of inter-office mail and plopped it on Bonnie's desk. On top of the stack was an envelope that Frank himself had sent to the boss that very morning. He had been curious about what the procedure was, so he watched.

Bonnie opened Frank's envelope, took out the five-page report, and gave each page a quick scan. Then, Frank's eyes widened in surprise as she did what she had been taught to do at business school. She took out a yellow marker and began highlighting the most important parts for the boss. Frank told the group how stunned he was, and stopped talking.

I could hear the wheels turning. They all knew it was true: the higher you go up the corporate ladder, the more people there are who handle your messages and highlight your reading material. I explained to the group that I believed that the person who did the writing should do the highlighting. And you highlight with subheads.

"Okay, you've made your point," the white-haired gent said. "Let's talk about subheads."

Whew! That was close.

Putting Subheads to Work

Following is another kind of business document, a sales letter. It uses subheads to great effect. It was written word for word (except for the names) by a participant in one of my corporate workshops. As he told me on the phone later, he used this letter to gain entry to a prospective customer he had been trying to reach—unsuccessfully—for months. The letter did the trick, and it led directly to his making a $6 million sale. How is that for real-world value? I share it with you so you can see for yourself how persuasive subheads can be.

October 17, 20XX

Ms. Norma Jean Baker
Trilkins & Co., Inc.
Fort Worth, TX 34567

Subject: How you can sell more refrigerators at a higher price.

Dear Norma Jean:
May I show you a way to sell more products at more profit to your company?

Imagine this scenario:

A refrigerator in one of the 500 Acme grocery stores becomes unplugged, or fails. As the temperature rises, an agent on a thermostat sends a warning to a monitoring station. A manager (who is on a smoke break at the back of the store) gets a pager message saying

- which refrigerator is down
- the current temperature
- how long he has to move the contents.

Acme grocery store cuts spoilage by a factor of 50 percent, saving $500 million a year. Trilkins becomes the exclusive provider of refrigeration equipment to Acme grocery stores.

How Trilkins & Co., Inc., Can Increase Sales Using Software Horizons Technology

1. Your products will pay for themselves in the savings they yield relative to your competitor's units.
2. Your products will stand out in the marketplace and generate tremendous publicity.
3. Software Horizons will work side by side with you in your sales process to large accounts.

Action Requested

Norma Jean, would you give me 30 minutes of your time during the first week in November? I'd like to discuss how we could incorporate Software Horizons agent technology into your products. I will call to schedule a time for our meeting.

Sincerely,
Archie Leach
OEM Group, Software Horizons

This is a sales letter, distinct from a cover letter, yet the principles of good writing are the same: a friendly, semi-formal tone; short sentences and paragraphs; a focus on the reader and her interests; and imaginative use of subheads to guide the reader's thoughts in the direction the writer wants to go. Note that for the first half of the letter the writer talks exclusively about the reader—he doesn't even mention his company or product until halfway down. The fact that it worked is incontrovertible, and proof enough that this style of writing is effective in the real world.

Table of Contents

This is required for any document over ten pages.

Executive Summary

This summary is a synopsis of the entire report in two or three pages. The summary emphasizes the genetic uniqueness of your company and suggests the nature of the matrix in which your enterprise will operate.

Here is the beginning of the summary I would write for Nurse's Choice. I want to engage the reader with friendly, focused prose, a sense of genuine excitement, and a conviction that while our feet are firmly on the ground, we dream big dreams.

EXECUTIVE SUMMARY

Until recently, Nurse's Choice (NC) has been a one-woman sideline business. Leigh Nielsen, a Registered Nurse and avid organic gardener and herbalist, discovered the winning formula for her hand crème after years of trial and error. The formula includes:

- Distilled water
- Aloe Vera gel
- Essential oil of choice
- Vitamin E
- Coconut oil
- Apricot mix
- Lanolin
- Beeswax
- Two other secret ingredients

The exact recipe and mixing process are patent-pending.

What gave Ms. Nielsen a sense of enormous potential for her product was the demand for it she discovered at the hospital where she is a surgical specialist. She shared her hand crème with a colleague one day and the colleague started raving about it to others. They in turn urgently requested that she make additional batches for them—price no object. Within days, word had spread throughout the hospital and virtually everyone on staff was using it and asking for more.

She has sold out every batch since and cannot make enough to satisfy demand. People are wrapping the crème as gifts and sending samples to colleagues at other hospitals.

With her hobby turning into a profitable business, Ms. Nielsen contacted her local SCORE organization of retired business professionals, who in turn recommended a team of active marketers. Earlier this year we formed a corporation, Nurse's Choice Inc., whose officers are:

- Joseph K. Altsheller, CEO
- W. Henry Ware, COO
- Ilona P. McQuillen, CFO
- Leigh Nielsen, Chairperson of the Board
- David X. Jenness, VP Sales

[NOTE: This Executive Summary can go on for several more pages, as desired, synopsizing the major elements of the full plan, as follows.]

The Financial Picture

It may take an experienced accountant to write this section properly and correctly. Since Nurse's Choice is an imaginary company and my financial data will be imaginary, they will be of no help to you. That said, I still recommend putting the financials up this early in your plan because after your executive summary, this is what investors really care about. I recommend, at minimum, you have the following data:

- *Profit and Loss Sheets* for the last several years, if you have them. If yours is a startup company, your accountant will guide you in preparing projections, including Current Assets, Fixed Assets, and Liabilities.
- *Quarterly Balance Sheets.*
- *Cash Flow Statement.*
- *Sales Forecasts* for the remainder of this fiscal year and for the next two years.
- *Advertising Plan* in detail, with projected figures.
- *Break Even Analysis* for each of the next five years.

For many more details on financing your enterprise please see Chapter 6.

Company Overview

The purpose of the overview is to settle in the reader's mind that you and your partners have thought through every aspect of the company and its ability to be profitable. It should easily occupy four to eight pages on its own.

Nurse's Choice, Inc., is a privately owned Delaware Corporation. It currently employs seven production workers, two truck drivers, three outside sales people, one inside sales person, two maintenance people, and five executives. With adequate financing we expect those figures to double within eighteen months. Within five years we project $6.3 million in annual sales, at which time we will take the company public. (And so on as necessary.)

The product is a deluxe hand crème. We use the European "crème" spelling to suggest a luxurious product, and indeed it is. The ingredients are all-natural and expensive. Nurse's Choice is the highest-priced hand cream or lotion on the market, and deservedly so.

Our facilities include a rented warehouse on the banks of the Merrimack River in Haverhill, Massachusetts; two panel-delivery trucks, one owned outright and one leased; a highly interactive website (NursesChoice.com); two Framitz-18 industrial mixers; one 20-foot conveyor belt; and a shipping/receiving dock. Our communications capacity includes high-speed internet and telephone cables; twenty-two laptop computers; an inbound telesales room; cell phones and PDAs with IM and internet access; and two GPS receivers. (And so on as necessary.)

There are five principal officers/owners of the company:

Leigh Nielsen, RN, is a fifteen-year medical veteran whose specialty is operating room nursing at Midtown Hospital. She holds a B.S. degree from Northeastern University, and is a Lieutenant Commander in the US Navy Reserve. While on active duty in Iraq, she performed under combat conditions and holds several commendations. She is the principal stockholder and serves as chair of the board of directors. (And so on as necessary.)

Joseph K. Altsheller, Attorney at Law, is Chief Executive Officer. He retired in 20XX from the Wall Street firm of Wood and Delacroix, where he was a senior partner specializing in industrial law. (And so on as necessary.)

David X. Jenness, B.A, is Vice President, Sales. He served in a similar capacity at Catalonia Lotions for seven years, where he was responsible for taking the company global. He opened up new markets for Catalonia in South America and Japan (and so on as necessary).

W. Henry Ware, MBA, is Chief Operating Officer. A graduate of the Wharton School, he has participated in the start-up of two other companies, taking both of them to public stock offerings with significantly improved value. This is Mr. Ware's first experience with a hand lotion, although he was a marketing director at Revlon for several years. (And so on as necessary.)

Ilona P. McQuillen, CPA, is Chief Financial Officer. (And so on as necessary.)

The Landscape

This may be your most important selling prose in the entire plan. It's here that you convince investors that you are realistic about your product and its place in the universe of similar products. You should have enough notes and research before you begin writing this section to fill around ten pages of good, high-energy prose.

THE LANDSCAPE IS TRENDING POSITIVE

The beauty business in general—worldwide—registers between $35 to $40 billion annually. Health clubs, gyms, spas, and vitamin use are all up and trending upward even faster over the next ten years.

The hand cream and lotion market in the United States is mature. The products are sold everywhere: drugstore chains, discount marts, big-box warehouse stores, supermarket chains, and variety stores. Eighty-five percent of purchasers are female and over 18. That said, research shows that women are open to new products in this area and are quite willing to try new products. There is little brand loyalty among women for hand lotions.

Among target female consumers, 53 percent moisturize their body daily, generally after bathing or showering. Even more—55 percent—moisturize their feet daily.

The new (and heretofore untapped) market is male. Use of these creams among men over 21 is increasing. In fact, men are turning to skincare products and appearance services in awe-inspiring numbers. And older men are leading the way. As the population ages, men are finding that a good-quality lotion eases cracks and scratches in hand skin. They are using facial cream in growing numbers too—a 15.2 percent increase since 20XX. Caring for one's skin is no longer a female-only concern.

Ironically, price is no issue for men over 35. Women use hand and face lotions routinely over the day, and tend to prefer a mid-price to low-price product. Women like to receive expensive lotions as gifts. Men tend to use a cream only once (after a shower and shave) and so prefer something longer-lasting and with a good clean scent. The difference in price is negligible (they believe) between a superior product and a discount product, like the difference in price between a boutique coffee and a store brand. And so they are susceptible to advertising suggesting that their skin is worth the slight increase in price.

There are at least two dozen high-quality brands in the United States and Europe. Three recent surveys (see the Appendix) suggest that people are "satisfied" or "somewhat satisfied" with these brands, but are open to other contenders. We have found virtually no brand loyalty, especially in the North American market. U.S. consumers see even the higher priced brands as commoditized, mass produced, and packaged by smart operators who go for the lowest common denominator and care little about specific ingredients. Women assume (when they think about it at all) that a perfume-like ingredient is added to improve the scent. Men prefer no scent, or something that reminds them of the outdoors. When probed about a scent that arises naturally from high-quality ingredients, with no artificial perfumes, both men and women expressed interest in at least trying it. And so on as necessary.

[Note: if I were writing this as a real plan, here are some other topics I would include in this section:

1. Clear trends
2. Predictions
3. Quotes from experts
4. Relevant quotes from recent marketing books
5. Legislation and legal issues
6. Red flags ahead
7. Clear reasons for optimism.]

The Market

Let's pick up where we left off in our sample plan. Your job here is to demonstrate that you know your market inside and out.

THE MARKET: ALL CATEGORIES ARE GROWING OR STABLE

We shall discuss four qualities of the market for Nurse's Choice: Domestic, International, Media, and Direct Sales.

The *domestic market* is huge. All of the major brands are tight-lipped about U.S. sales, preferring to talk in "millions" or "multi-millions." Of course, these companies have stellar distribution and years of branding to build on. Nevertheless, loyalty is so thin as to be virtually nonexistent. (And so on as necessary.)

The *international market* is a much greater challenge; we shall attempt to penetrate it only after several years of strong domestic sales. Europeans and South Americans, especially, find little or no cachet in an American brand of lotion. If it doesn't originate in Paris, so the thinking goes, it is strictly for colonials.

That said, international sophisticates quickly give the nod to American products that perform a practical function. A hand balm from dairy farmers; toothpaste from Maine or Vermont; insect repellent; antiseptic cream—all do well among internationals. We shall, in short time, achieve placement on pharmacy shelves alongside Tom's of Maine and other well-known practical products from America.

For *media*, think new and inexpensive. The Internet is a glorious resource that we shall take full advantage of. To begin, we shall offer the usual array of discounts, coupons, website specials, and banner advertising.

Chris Anderson, author of *The Long Tail*, says this about the dynamic new markets the Web is revealing: "For the first time in history, hits and niches are on equal economic footing, both just entries in a database called up on demand, both equally worthy of being carried. Suddenly, popularity no longer has a monopoly on profitability." (And so on as necessary.)

Direct Sales offers our most lucrative outreach. As Ms. Nielsen's original experience suggests, when people try our hand crème, they go crazy (so to speak). They must have it. They demand to know where they can buy it. They demand some on the spot for immediate use. They become indignant to find they cannot have more until Ms. Nielsen's day off next week. In short, people love it instantly. Given such facts, we intend to sample our hand crème widely and liberally. Once people try it, they tend to buy it with little regard to price.

We will begin with a direct-response postcard to the staffs at hospitals and medical offices, offering a free trial. We will place sample jars in rural areas for farmers and construction workers to try. (And so on as necessary.)

The Competition

Never underestimate your competition, and never minimize the threat of competitors in a business plan. If you do, financiers will chuckle as they toss your plan into the nearest waste bin.

THE COMPETITION: A MATURE MARKET WEAKENS COMPETITION

The real value to a newcomer in a mature market is that competitors expect little or no innovation.

Nurse's Choice is truly innovative at the high end. Competitors expect to fight for sales at the lowest price point—the place where most innovation flourishes. The high end, however, is open territory. Given the purity and naturalness of its ingredients, Nurse's Choice cannot compete over price points. It would be like offering a discount on a Rolls Royce. NC costs what it costs because the ingredients are so demonstrably pure and effective.

Given that, we consider our product to have only three true competitors. (If this were a real product, I would provide here an exhaustive study of the real competition. I want my reader to take away a strong sense that I have done my homework and have a firm grasp on the challenges ahead. If I use subheads properly, readers can skip around in this multi-page discussion freely and easily.)

Personnel

This section should contain a study of each critical position, and indicate where you might save money by hiring entry-level and part-time workers or outsourcing work altogether. If necessary, discuss how you will fill key, critical positions and how much money it will take to do so.

Sales and Promotion

In this section, outline your marketing strategy and methods for getting products in the hands of consumers.

SALES AND PROMOTION: WE CANNOT DISCOUNT OUR PRODUCT INTO PEOPLE'S HANDS; WE MUST SELL IT.

The success of Nurse's Choice is driven by sales representatives, both inside and outside.

We see an outside sales force as the heart of our company. This product requires a classic sales rep, sample case in hand and a warm personality to go with the product. NC is above all else personal. You rub this on your skin. You breathe in its healthful aromas and you feel its silky texture with your fingers. People have all tried hand cream at one time or another. They think they understand such a product and are prepared to be "underwhelmed" with any new lotion. That's why personal trial is paramount, and why a sales rep is the key to trial.

We will invest in our sales force. They will be top performers, and will be compensated as professionals who understand their value to the organization. Nurse's Choice is hands-on, so to speak, not arm's length. When people try it, they will buy it. And they will try it mostly at the gentle urging of someone they instinctively trust.

Our sales reps will start by calling on medical facilities, from hospitals to private practices. This is our core market, where the grass is greenest. They will then expand their range to department stores, drugstores, boutiques such as perfume shops and women's clothing stores, and men's clothing stores.

[This should get specific and territorial for several pages.]

[The next sections talk about inbound telemarketing, outbound telemarketing, direct response campaigns, and Internet plans.]

Appendix

The Appendix is often overlooked, or simply an afterthought. But its value is clear: This is a repository of everything that could possibly help your capital-generating goals, from graphs and maps to marketing surveys and even transcripts of interviews and conversations.

If I may use such language, the Appendix is where you "show off" your company and your own due diligence. You can impress readers here. You can be imaginative and even off message, as long as it showcases your company's strengths.

For Nurse's Choice, I might write a piece if time allows on the history of hand and body creams. It is not strictly germane to my plan, but it might intrigue an investor sufficiently to get a nod in my direction. I might also include some hard data on how proper washing of hands prevents the spread of germs. Human beings wash their hands far less frequently than they should. As this message becomes more widespread in the culture, the care of hands then becomes even more important.

I might include medical research data on how germs are transmitted from surfaces and in the air and from people to ourselves. I might include the top line of studies that show how repeated washing depletes epidermal cells of their moisture and how high-quality lotions replace that moisture.

I would include any item that the reader would find interesting, with two caveats:

- It must help to make my case for my product.
- It cannot take me beyond that magical forty to forty-five page range for the complete plan.

4

Edit for Power: The Hard Part

The best headlines are those that appeal to the reader's self interest, that is, headlines based on readers' benefits. They offer readers something they want—and can get from you.

John Caples, Copywriter's Hall of Fame

Remember the painting analogy I offered in Chapter 3? Preparing to write is worth 50 percent of your writing time. It's like preparing for a paint job. Writing the first draft is worth 20 percent of your time and resembles painting the surface with that lovely new color. Now it's time to clean up, accounting for the last 30 percent of your writing task. And this is where your hard work pays off in a clean, compelling piece of writing—one that will help you get the money or whatever else you seek to move your business forward.

I also suggested in the previous chapter that creating the first draft is a right-brain task: creative, imaginative, expressive. Now it's time for your rock-solid left hemisphere to step up and take over. Editing, or revising, or rewriting is essentially logical work. You now apply cold reason to the work that you just wrote while in a warm creative mood. And it's here that you will strategically shape your document to win your objective.

The Actor's Studio in New York built a worldwide reputation on one central idea: Acting is reacting. Actors enhance believability when they listen to the lines that another actor gives them and react to the message in those lines.

Similarly, writing is re-writing.

I've never heard of a professional writer who submits a first draft. It is unthinkable. Writers labor over subsequent drafts, putting in and taking out commas, changing a dime word to a dollar word and back again, rearranging paragraphs, and sweating the details. And so should you.

If you can stand another analogy, writing the first draft is like a sculptor pressing together giant slabs of clay. Once all your working material is in place, then you can shape it into a beautiful statue. Writing the first draft is simply getting all of your material together. When you know you have every critical idea on paper, you can relax and start shaping those ideas into something that others will want to read.

Ideally, you'll be able to put a day or two between the finish of your first draft and the start of editing. You'll be amazed at how many errors you'll see right off. Unfortunately for writers, our brains tend to see on the page what we intended, rather than what we actually wrote. When you put some time between the first and subsequent drafts, it is as if you are now looking at a first draft someone else wrote. It's also why I recommend you have a colleague proofread your final draft before you send it off.

TOOLS FOR SHAPING YOUR PROSE

Writing the first draft should not be the hard part for you. It's the easy part, where you just sit and write and let the ideas flow. Editing is the hard part. That's when you turn raw ideas into powerful thinking that helps the reader to see it your way. Good editing requires good tools. Here are some that will help make the work easier.

1. An editing checklist: a roadmap to make reading your prose easier.
2. A primer on active versus passive voice.
3. Transitions for flow and polish.
4. Parallel sentence structures.
5. Clichés and other writing pitfalls.
6. Graphics to enhance the reader's understanding of your ideas.

With your entire first draft now available to you, skim across it briefly from start to finish. Your task now is to apply logic to what was formerly a purely creative enterprise. Look for big-picture issues first and put off the small stuff until later. I say this because many of your errors will disappear when you cut and trim.

It's time to edit. Editing is far different from proofreading. Proofreading is merely the search for errors such as misspellings and improper capitalizations. Editing is essentially starting over by using the raw material of your first draft and reshaping it into a persuasive document. Editing requires a macro-view and micro-tinkering. It's hard work.

To help, here is that classic left-brain tool, the checklist:

EDITING CHECKLIST: A ROADMAP TO MAKE READING YOUR PROSE EASIER

1. Fix these first:

__ Is my structure clear to a disinterested reader?
__ Do my ideas progress from one to the other logically?
__ Do I begin each section with a vigorous explanatory paragraph that makes my point of view clear?

___ Is my overall tone appropriate for my reader? (I suggest you write a formal business proposal using the same style I use in this book, i.e., minimum contractions, minimum jargon, but nonetheless personable.)

___ Are my arguments convincing?

___ Is my plan the appropriate length and in the appropriate format?

2. Fix these next:

___ Is my viewpoint consistent, or do I keep shifting from "I" to "you" to "us"?

___ Have I made it crystal clear for the reader what my product/service is and what my plans are for the business?

___ If I were the reader, would I invest money in the company described in my plan?

___ Are my transitions from one idea to another clear?

___ Is the layout visually attractive?

___ Does the plan look uncluttered and professional?

___ Are there places where I can use graphics rather than prose to make my point sharper or to enhance the reader's understanding?

3. Fix these last:

___ Are my sentences short and crisp? (Ten to twenty words is a good range. More than that and you are blathering.)

___ Are my paragraphs no longer than five typed lines?

___ Are there no spelling errors or typos?

___ Do I write consistently in the active voice?

___ Am I specific rather than vague? For example, "We spent several weeks developing a primary prospect list" is not as good as "We spent 27 days developing a primary prospect list."

___ Are my subheads and lists parallel in structure?

___ Do I know the rule regarding each punctuation mark I have used?

___ Do I use strong verbs with few adjectives?

___ Have I eliminated all uses of "very"?

___ Is my prose personable, tactful, and respectful?

___ Do verbs agree with subjects?

___ Do pronouns agree with antecedents?

___ Is my writing positive at all times?

Everything You Could Possibly Want to Know about Active and Passive Voice

Let's recall my advice about writing the first draft: Write quickly and in a warm mode, ignoring the niceties of mechanics and spelling. Just get it all down as fast as you can. That's using your right brain efficiently. And when it comes to editing, give your right brain a few hours off and use your left-brain skills for smoothing out the work.

The most common stylistic error I see is overuse of the passive voice. It has become the voice of choice for business writing in America, and I am

To Print or Not to Print?

There are talented people of good will on both sides of this issue.

Should you print out your first draft and work from the hard copy? Or should you join the twenty-first century and work on your first draft while it's on the screen? This is not a small concern.

I was conducting some training sessions at one of the world's largest computer manufacturers recently and brought up a similar issue to the group regarding sales letters. One bright young wiseacre raised his hand and said, "Dennis, I'm sure we have a printer or two somewhere around here, but I really don't know where."

I took his point. Interactivity is the name of the game. People simply will no longer pass around a hard copy for comments when they can make wholesale changes on *your* work with just a few clicks and a change in font color.

My point of view is based on the fragility of ideas. They are easier to kill than butterflies, especially in the nascent stage. If you start e-mailing around half-formed ideas and weak expressions in a first draft, people will feel free to change them. So make sure the draft you pass around is as good as you can make it. People will still make changes, but you will have fulfilled your obligation as a writer to make your published draft as good as it can be.

I advocate printing out your first draft—rather than working on screen—for five reasons.

1. A hard copy is real. One takes it seriously.
2. You can get a much better sense of the big picture when you spread those pages out on your desk. You can catch flaws in structure and design more easily, whereas scrolling up and down on screen makes this difficult.
3. This is your work and yours only. The best writing comes from a single vantage point, not from a committee. Printing it out reinforces that in your mind. (Thomas Jefferson wrote the Declaration of Independence. The other Founders simply discussed it and signed it.)
4. You are now looking at a different document in a different medium from that in which you wrote it; that fresh look will help you smooth out the rough spots.
5. You are looking at the document in the same medium in which the ultimate reader will see it, assuming you send a hard copy rather than an electronic attachment. Is bold good enough? Or should you increase the font size as well? Is the flow of topics obvious and useful to the reader? It is the best way I know of to put yourself in the reader's place.

For these reasons I also advocate sending a final-edit hard copy to your primary reader. If she prefers receiving an attachment, so be it. But a printed document has heft and existence. It must be dealt with. It is the medium of reality.

on a one-person crusade to promote active voice as the default mode. (Actually I'm far from the only person advocating the active voice, but I'm the only writer you are reading at this moment.)

Please understand that writing in the passive voice is perfectly legal. You may write in the passive voice all day long, if you choose, and receive not a whimper of protest from grammarians. Lawyers, for example, write almost exclusively in passive voice. The same is true for laboratory technicians and scientists. They often have solid reasons for writing in passive. That being said, too many business writers use passive voice for the wrong reasons—they're too lazy to write in the active voice, or—worst reason of all—the boss prefers passive.

I encourage you to write in the active voice—except on those rare occasions when passive is preferable—for some important reasons.

What Is "Voice"?

Voice is a function of two of your most important choices: the subject and the verb. If you decide that the subject of the sentence is doing the action, then your verb will be in the active voice. If you decide that the subject receives the action, then you'll choose passive voice. Please note that voice has nothing to do with verb tense. You may write actively in any tense. For example, past tense:

"The pilot steered the ship hard to port."

The pilot is the subject, and has performed the action.
You may write passively in any tense. For example, present tense:

"The ship is steered hard to port by the pilot."

The ship is the subject, and is receiving the action.

Active Voice	Passive Voice
Jenny catered the dinner.	The dinner was catered by Jenny.
The actor rehearsed his lines.	The lines were rehearsed by the actor.

I recommend default use of the active voice because it is:

- Stronger
- Shorter
- Livelier
- More involving

A business document in the active voice, using short sentences and short paragraphs, has an urgency and forthrightness about it that no other style can match.

On the other hand, passive voice has its place as well. Good writers choose passive when active would be inappropriate or misleading.

I ran across a fine example of this while I was teaching a technical-writing workshop at a government forensic laboratory recently. We were on the subject of active and passive voice when one of the crime-scene investigators shared this sentence with us. She had that morning included it in a report sent to the District Attorney: "Two blue fibers from the victim's coat were discovered on the suspect's shoe."

This is excellent use of passive voice. Why? Because the writer is putting the most important element in front. True, the two blue fibers are not generating any action. However, the person who did generate the action in this sentence, the unmentioned lab technician, is irrelevant, especially to the prosecutor. What's most important is that the two blue fibers were discovered, and that they were on the suspect's shoe. Those two blue fibers will put a killer away. Therefore the sentence should begin with them.

Some Passive-Voice Guidelines

Use passive voice in these circumstances:

- To avoid identifying the doer of the action (e.g., "An error was made in announcing the gate change.").
- When the doer of the action is unknown (e.g., "The deeds were notarized in Santa Fe.").
- When the doer of the action is less important than the receiver (e.g., "The newly revised contracts have just been released by the company's legal department.").

I object to passive voice only when writers use it by default, without thinking that maybe active voice would have been preferable. Here are some typical sentences that are unnecessarily passive:

- Any garbage must be placed in appropriate containers.
- The floor should be washed down and squeegeed.
- Care should be taken while sterilizing laboratory equipment.
- If power is not available, an extension cord must be run from the equipment storage room into the S.U.L.

These are all real sentences from operations manuals. Active voice would make them stronger:

- Place garbage in appropriate containers.
- Please wash down and squeegee the floor.
- Take care while sterilizing laboratory equipment.
- If power is not available, run an extension cord from the equipment storage room into the S.U.L.

Some writers feel that passive voice is more polite and less imperative. To them, "place garbage in appropriate containers" or "wash and squeegee the floor" sounds dictatorial. My response is that "please" goes a long way to mitigate any such suggestion.

Transitions: When Your Prose Needs More "Flow"

Transitions are another open secret of professional writers. There are two types of transitions:

1. Words or phrases
2. Sentences

Transitions guide your reader from one thought to another. They are like mile markers, showing the way. Words or phrases that function as transitions include *however, moreover, therefore, on the other hand, for the most part,* and so on. They typically are used at the beginning of a sentence. They are useful for signaling the reader that we are continuing in the same direction (*moreover*) or changing direction (*however*). They alert the reader to an important point (*interestingly, ironically*) and locate the reader in time or place (*formerly, nearby, first, third*). If you can remember to put in a proper transition where one is called for, your prose will take on that elusive "flow" that bosses seem to value so highly.

Sentence transitions from one paragraph to the next are more complex. You don't want to use them between every paragraph, but they serve to summarize before moving on, whenever a summary is called for.

For example, consider the following two paragraphs, with a sentence transition at the start of the second paragraph:

> A good business plan captures the reader's interest from the start. Some begin with the grand idea first, hitting the reader between the eyes with the sheer boldness of the concept. Others take something of a running start, beginning with a small but intriguing concept and ramping up quickly and confidently to a strong pinnacle—the central idea upon which hangs a multi-million dollar enterprise.
>
> *While both the bold start and the slow build are useful strategies, the shrewd entrepreneur considers the reader in deciding which style is better.* Venture capital firms, for example, attract people who have a bold approach to life. On the other hand, commercial banks appeal to people who are security minded and plan for the long haul.

Sign in an Advertising Agency Conference Room

"There is no human desire—not for food, for shelter, for sex, for love—greater than the desire to change what someone else has written."
[Of course, the sign has all sorts of corrections penciled in on it.]

Table 4.1
Active Ingredients in Nurse's Choice Hand Creme

Ingredient	Source	Benefit
Aloe	Plant	Heals skin surface
Lanolins	Wool coats of sheep	Adherence
Coconut Oil	Tree	Soothes emotions

Parallelism: A Crucial Part of Left-Brain Logic

Parallel structure, in your prose and in your graphics, is a clear signal to the reader that you are in charge and know what you are doing. Nonparallel structure is a sign of weakness or lack of attention to detail. Parallel structure is essentially balance. If, for example, you have used verb-verb-verb to begin the first three items in a list, then you need to use a verb to begin the fourth. Here is a typical example of nonparallel writing: "At the sales training workshops she learned how to conduct a sales interview, discern personality types, and the art of customer-focused selling."

Parallel errors occur mostly in lists. You can see the imbalance if you put the items in bullets:

At the sales training workshops she learned how to:

- *Conduct* a sales interview.
- *Discern* personality types.
- *And the art* of customer-focused selling.

The structure here is obviously verb-verb-noun. Not good. We need a third verb, as in this fix: "At the sales training workshops she learned how to conduct a sales interview, discern personality types, and practice the art of customer-focused selling." Now the structure is conduct-discern-practice. All verbs, all in balance.

Try another one: "The community college offers evening classes, child care arrangements, and the teachers really care about their students."

This is slightly out of parallel. A straightforward noun in the third item will fix it: "The community college offers evening classes, child care arrangements, and teachers who really care about their students."

Parallelism applies to tables and charts as well.

The Lanolins row is clearly not parallel with the other two (Table 4.1). Making it strictly parallel will ease a reader's sense of balance and help to give him confidence in your work (Table 4.2).

Cliches: Avoid Them Like the Plague

Oops! "Like the plague" is a cliché. Let's try this: "Writers wouldn't touch 'em with a ten-foot pole." Oops! Clichés pop up where you least expect them. The damage they do is silent, under the surface, but it is damage none the less.

Table 4.2
"Parallel" Version of the Active Ingredients Table

Ingredient	Source	Benefit
Aloe	Plant	Heals skin surface
Lanolin	Sheep Wool	Adheres to epidermis
Coconut Oil	Tree	Soothes emotions

A cliché is an expression so overused that it no longer has juice—or life—or real meaning. If you use too many clichés in your work, the reader will start to wonder how original you are after all. Early on in its career, a cliché had a strong, juice-filled meaning. For example, "playing both ends against the middle" comes to American English straight from the Old West of the 1870s. It came from saloon denizens who played Faro, a card game similar to today's Blackjack and dealt by the likes of Wyatt Earp and Doc Holliday.

Here's a whole paragraph of nothing but clichés:

> In reference to the paradigm shift brought into necessity by circumstances beyond our control, please be advised that pursuant to our conversation we acknowledge receipt of the above referenced report. Enclosed please find as per your request our response. Please do not hesitate to call with your questions.

(In a workshop, one of my participants slapped her forehead and exclaimed, "Holy smoke, I just wrote that this morning in a memo!")

Now let's think about some of these expressions.

"Please be advised." What on earth does that mean? Please be in a state of advisement? Stand by because now I'm going to say something? If, like me, you're not sure what it means, then don't say it.

"Pursuant to our conversation ..." Would you ever say that in real life? Would you sit down with a colleague over coffee and say, "Hey, Joshua, pursuant to our last conversation ..."? I think not. So why would you write that?

"Please do not hesitate to call ..." What does that mean? Why would someone hesitate to call? This is America in the twenty-first century and we don't hesitate to do anything anymore. The only way this expression works today is to turn it around: "I'm going on vacation tomorrow, so please hesitate to call."

Here are some more tried-and-true clichés. See if you are guilty of using any of them in the past six months:

- At that point in time
- Subsequent to
- It may interest you to know
- As plain as day
- Walk a mile in my shoes
- Don't go there

- Sharp as a bowling ball
- Throw the baby out with the bath water
- Last but not least
- In the event that
- It's all good
- Think outside the box

Now there's a good one: think outside the box. It became a cliché about mid-June 2000, but we still use it to suggest, ironically enough, that one should be more creative.

When Shakespeare had Richard III shout "My kingdom for a horse!" it was a fearsome moment in theater history—the hunchback king storming about the stage and raging against the Fate that will destroy him. Now it's just a cliché. When Shakespeare had an anarchist, Dick the Butcher, in Henry VI, Part 2, say to his fellow conspirators: "The first thing we do, let's kill all the lawyers," the audience must have doubled up laughing at the freshness and audacity of the idea. Now it's just a cliché. (Shakespeare was a ready client of lawyers; the line does not express his own sentiments at all. Dick the Butcher was looking to mow down the last barricade standing between himself and chaos.)

Your reader is looking for original, action-based, juice-filled ideas. Don't disappoint her with old, dried up, prune-wrinkled clichés.

GRAPHICS ENHANCE COMPREHENSION

Now that you have your prose document in order, it's time to enhance the power of your ideas with some well-designed and well-placed graphics.

Many effective business plans and proposals contain colorful graphics. A well-conceived graphic can take the place of hundreds of words and make your point even stronger. For example, I could take a page or two of prose to describe how a hand cream helps skin cells to heal. Or I could show the reader an illustration, complete with call-outs and a caption.

Graphics are visuals. Our brains process visuals faster and remember them longer than we process and remember prose.

Since modern software gives us so many ways to show data graphically, writers must determine the best choice according to the reader's needs. Here are some guidelines:

1. Choose the best type of graphic for your data.
2. Explain its meaning within the text.
3. Put the graphic close to its first mention in the text.
4. Give each graphic a number and title.
5. Write an information-rich caption that helps readers to see the meaning clearly.
6. Provide enough white space to avoid clutter.

Let's examine these more closely one at a time. First, see Table 4.3 on which I built most of these graphics.

Table 4.3
Annual Skin Lotion Expenditures in North America in Millions of Dollars
(these figures are fictional for modeling purposes only)

Year	Women	Men	Medical	Industrial
6/30/1998	$195.00	$14.00	$22.30	$7.50
6/30/1999	$201.00	$15.00	$22.40	$7.40
6/30/2000	$202.00	$17.30	$22.70	$7.90
6/30/2001	$198.00	$19.00	$25.50	$8.80
6/30/2002	$223.00	$18.90	$26.00	$8.70
6/30/2003	$228.70	$21.00	$29.50	$9.20
6/30/2004	$231.00	$24.00	$29.90	$11.40
6/30/2005	$229.40	$27.70	$31.00	$14.00
6/30/2006	$258.00	$29.00	$32.70	$14.00
6/30/2007	$261.60	$29.50	$37.00	$16.20

Choose the Best Type for Your Data

Don't just take your data and have Excel spit out any old graphic. There is a time and place for each:

Type	*Shows*
Line drawing	Detail when realism is not critical
Photograph	Realistic detail
Pie chart	Macro percentages (see Figure 4.1)
Bar or column graph	Groupings of data and micro percentages (see Figure 4.2)
Line graph	Trends over time (see Figure 4.3)
Map	Positions or locations
Table	Data in context, using rows and columns (see Table 4.3)
Gantt chart	Shows actions on one axis and timeframe on the other (see Figure 4.4)
Organizational chart	People and relative relationships
Network diagram	Relationships of people or activities, including slack time and delays (see Figure 4.5)

Figure 4.1
Pie Chart

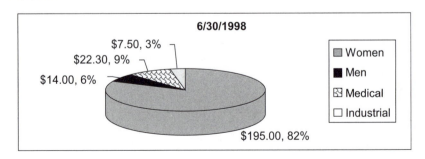

Figure 4.2
Bar Graph

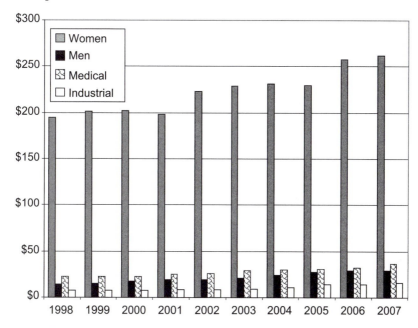

Figure 4.3
Line Graph

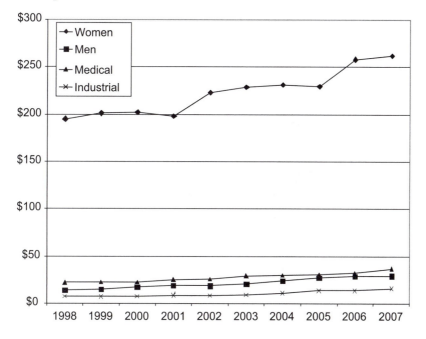

Figure 4.4
Gantt Chart

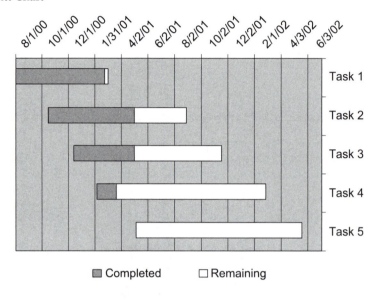

Figure 4.5
A Sample Network Diagram

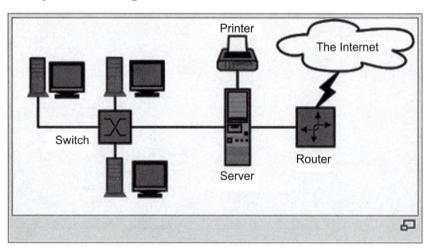

Explain Its Meaning within the Text

You must interpret all graphics for the reader, and you do it in two ways. First, in the text itself discuss the context of the graphic and precisely what it shows or proves. Second, in a caption discuss or explain the single most important point you want the reader to take away from that graphic. All graphics deserve captions, as people can't resist reading captions. I consider it a dereliction of a writer's duty to display a graphic without an information-rich caption underneath.

Put the Graphic Close to Its First Mention in the Text

Readers will be most interested in the graphic just after you first mention it. I suggest you follow a simple format:

- Introduce the graphic in a short paragraph or two.
- Present the graphic.
- Provide a rich caption beneath the graphic that stresses the one or two most important points to be gleaned from the graphic.
- In following paragraphs, explain how readers can best interpret the graphic and repeat the main ideas within it.

Give Each Graphic a Number and Title

Good technical-writing format allows you to separate graphics from all other elements in your document. Most authorities advise identifying each with a number and title. For example:

Figure 5.7: Allocation of advertising resources for the next fiscal year showing emphasis on Web promotion.

The "5" is the chapter number. The "7" identifies it as the seventh graphic within the chapter. And the title should contain the most important factual nugget within the graphic.

If you do not use chapters, then a simple numerical and alphabetical system will do. For example:

Figure 3.A: Dry skin cell close to the epidermis.
Figure 3.B: Same cell with Nurse's Choice application.
And so on.

Write an Information-Rich Caption That Helps Readers to See the Meaning Clearly

For fifty years, the direct-response industry has been churning out research on what works and what doesn't work to enhance readership. This research is definitive and incontrovertible; business writers ignore it at their peril.

For example, we know that color improves readership over black-and-white significantly, up to 50 percent. We know that enclosing a Business Reply Card enhances response rates, even though few prospects use the BRC, preferring instead to click on the Web or make a phone call. And we know that long copy works better than short copy in generating response rates—every time, and in the face of all logic suggesting that shorter is better. These facts are not debatable.

Further, research tells us that there are three elements in any business document that people will almost certainly read:

- A headline or subject line.
- A caption.
- A P.S. after the signature in a letter.

This is not a book on direct-response writing. If you want a good one, I suggest *Direct Marketing* by George Duncan.

It is important to note that a caption is virtually guaranteed to generate readership. People cannot resist captions in the same way they cannot resist chocolate. Captions, by their very nature and location beneath a graphic, tempt us to read them, and few of us can tie ourselves to the mast, Ulysses-like, to prevent yielding to temptation. Therefore, please use a caption beneath every graphic in your document.

And make that caption rich in persuasiveness. Now that you know they will almost certainly read it, make it good. Stress the value of the information. Sell whatever benefit shows up in the graphic.

By the way, the fact that most people will read the P.S. after the signature in a letter is just one of those quirks of human nature for which there is little accounting. But you should take advantage of that knowledge, too, in every business letter you write.

Provide Enough White Space to Avoid Clutter

White space is another of those secrets-in-plain-sight that direct-response copywriters use to make us reach for our checkbooks.

The next time you get a piece of "junk" mail, examine it before you throw it away. (As a direct-response copywriter myself, I believe that junk mail is simply direct mail sent to the wrong person.) You will notice that, among many other details, the main letter contains almost as much white space as it does text. White space connotes professionalism, lack of anxiety, confidence, and skill. It allows the reader's eyes to rest along the way, thus extending the time a reader is willing to stay with you.

A COROLLARY

While we are on the subject of readership, you should also know that a classic serif type face, such as New Times Roman or Clearface, is much easier to read than a sans-serif face. Serif type wins every readership test ever given. A serif is that little squiggle or line detail you see on the ends of letters, such as this:

A or S

Sans-serif, of course, lacks the squiggle, such as this:

A or S

A sans-serif face looks more contemporary and technical than a serif face. But so what? You want readership, so use a serif face. Please.

5

Prepare for Success: Develop a Realistic Marketing Plan

It's supposed to be hard! If it wasn't hard, everyone would do it. The hard is what makes it great.

Tom Hanks as Jimmy Dugan in *A League of Their Own*

Your plan to market and sell your product or service is the heart of any larger business plan. A business, after all, is an organization that has customers. Your ideas about seeking out and winning customers will be of major interest to any investor, as well as to your board of directors and employees.

Because there are hundreds of such plans available for you to examine on the Internet, I thought the best value to you would be to provide a fill-in-the-blank format that you could use as a brainstorming and thinking tool.

The original of this marketing and sales plan was provided by Michael Irwin, marketing director at Adventures in Advertising, Inc. Mike's professional achievements include Master Advertising Specialist (MAS) and Certified Advertising Specialist (CAS). AIA is a franchisor with over 400 franchisees who sell promotional products. Mike provides this plan to franchise owners (entrepreneurs all!) to help them plan their businesses better and increase their profits. I am grateful for his contribution. I have kept his original structure, but shortened it and altered the descriptions to suit a more general readership.

MARKETING AND SALES PLAN

This section will include philosophy and objectives of your business, the kind of image you intend to portray, the strengths, weaknesses, opportunities and threats you must consider, and your expectations for the future.

Description

Any good marketing plan begins with a description of your business. This description should serve a wide variety of readers, from partners and key employees to investors and newspaper reporters. It is the foundation for every business decision you make.

- Describe your product or service.
- Discuss your general philosophy of doing business.
- Define the actual business you are in. For example, let's say you are in the data storage business. You could define it only by servers and gigabytes, support staff, and sales. A better way might be to define it by what your business means to your customers: peace of mind, compliance with regulations, improved client service, and so on.

Image Objectives

- How is your business or industry perceived in the market today?
- How do you want it to be perceived in the future?
- Do you wish to change the image? Why? How will you achieve this change?
- If the image change requires operational changes, explain them and the impact they will have on your daily internal operations. Consider:

    - Products/services offered
    - Past promotional objectives/initiatives
    - Past marketing and branding content
    - Sales organization and strategy
    - Support staff roles
    - Client/prospect perception
    - Past target markets

SWOT

SWOT, remember, means Strengths, Weaknesses, Opportunities, and Threats. Address the factors that have the most influence on your marketing and sales plan. Describe the most critical aspects of your plan, focusing on how you will leverage your strengths to take advantage of perceived opportunities. Next, focus on how you will respond to threats and how you will compensate for known weaknesses. Factors to consider:

- Your special or unique abilities and areas of expertise.
- Changes in the economy.
- Requirement for (or loss of) key personnel.
- Changes in government policies or regulations.
- Social or environmental changes.

Strengths:
Weaknesses:
Opportunities:
Threats:

The Future

Project any organizational changes, such as growth in personnel count or economic downturn in your area. Discuss any new products, services, or business concepts that may have some likelihood of affecting your business in the near future.

Market

This section will describe the general characteristics of the market segments that you believe have the most need for your products/services. Please consider any environmental influences, the needs of the marketplace, the geographic, demographic, and psychographic characteristics of your target market(s), how you will qualify prospects, and the kind of competition you believe you will be facing.

Description

Discuss generally the markets you want to compete in. List viable market segments. Can you penetrate those markets? For example, you might divide your potential market into three major categories: For-Profit, Not-For-Profit, and Government agencies. You could divide your market among the industries prevalent in your area, such as Healthcare, Education, High-Tech, and Construction. Which of these segments can you market to? Break them down further by:

- Local, regional, and national.
- Buying power.
- Ability to use what you offer.
- Extent of need for what you offer.
- Speed of purchase decision process.
- And so on.

Factors to consider:

- Extent of market.
- General description of segments.
- Current vs. new customers.
- Size of typical prospect.
- Prospect profitability.
- Current ability of prospect to use product or service.
- Prospect's incentive to buy.
- Prospect's decision-making process.

Market Segments

Specify, with specific names, which of the potential market segments described above represent the primary targets you will be selling to, and why.

Factors to consider:

- Their immediate need for your product/service.
- Your area of expertise, knowledge, or comfort.
- Purchasing power.
- Accessibility.
- Willingness to make a decision.

Name these segments specifically:

- Name
- Name
- Name

Prospects

Objectives

Who are your buyers? Why would they want an offering like yours? What would their objectives be in using your products or services?

Factors to consider:

- Purchaser's job title.
- Secondary influencers of the purchase decision.
- Typical initiatives of that buyer.
- How the buyer measures benefits.
- Customization, if any.

Name at least three objectives customers would have in using your product or service.

1.
2.
3.

Segmentation

List the categories within the broader marketing categories for your products or services. For example, for my Nurse's Choice hand crème the market segments might be:

- Pharmacies
- Hospital gift shops
- Sporting goods stores
- And so on

Now list three or four categories of your own:

1.
2.
3.

Alternatives

Describe what alternatives your prospects have to achieve their objectives, and WHY your prospects or customers should buy your offering.

Prospects

Name half a dozen companies or potential customers for your product or service:

- Name
- Name
- Name
- Name
- Name
- Name

Competition

Please summarize your competition as a group. How are you positioned as one of the competitors: low, medium, high? Describe the strongest competitors and their offerings, and explain why they are so strong. If your business plan includes tactics that are a direct response to one of more of the competitors, describe these tactics and explain why you expect them to be effective.

My strongest competitors are:

-
-

Marketing and Sales Strategy

In this section you will describe your marketing and sales strategy as it relates to your offering(s) and your desired image and positioning. Let's define "positioning" as the slot you own in the customer's mind. For example, Volvo owns the slot called "safe" in a prospect's mind.

Products/Services

First, list your products or services:

-
-
-

Value

For each product or service, explain why it is of value to a purchaser and set that value in measurable terms. Consider key advantages such as measurability, targetability, utilitarian worth, shelf life, and number of impressions.

Packaging

Describe your plan for marketing and selling your offering as a packaged good. What benefits will the package provide to your customers and prospects? Your own marketing efforts? What will be your resources?

Pricing

When competing in a normal environment you must offer your products or services at prices comparable to your competition. You may price your offerings higher than the competition if you can differentiate them with unique features or if you can focus on a niche market that you are somehow better able to serve.

Factors to consider:

- Market penetration objectives.
- Strength of competitors.
- Measurable value of your offering.
- Prospect's sensitivity to price vs. product value.

Promotion

Describe your promotion strategy. How will you go to market? What image do you plan to project? What image is your competition likely to try to force on you? What is the essence of your brand?

Image

Describe how you and your brand are perceived in the marketplace today and how you want to be perceived in the future. If you are changing your image, explain why and how you expect to achieve the change.

Factors to consider:

- Emotional appeal.
- Customer satisfaction.
- Degree to which it solves customer's problem.
- Feature comparison to competition.
- Price versus quality.

Publicity

How do you intend to generate interest? What form will your publicity take? When will the publicity occur, or over how long a time frame?

Factors to consider:

- Self-promotions and campaigns.
- Press releases.
- Media kits.
- Endorsements from customers or experts.
- Testimonials.
- Involvement in networking groups.
- Local/national news articles.

Advertising

You are looking for high exposure per dollar invested. Describe each form of advertising you plan to use, the market or accounts it is aimed at, the kind of outside help (if any) you will need, estimated costs and returns.

Factors to consider:

- Reach.
- Frequency.
- Your brand identity.
- Budget for first year.

Objectives

Describe short-term (one to two years) and long-term (three to five years) sales and profit objectives for your business.

Sales

Convincing your prospects to buy requires the right sales approach and commitment. How will you sell your offerings? If you use sales-people, how will they be compensated?

Factors to consider:

- Sales method.
- Length of sales cycle.
- Training for sales reps.

Sales Philosophy

Good salespeople have one objective in mind—close the sale. This is what you want, but only if it is done in such a way as to profitably satisfy the customers' requirements. This section should describe the ethics and procedures and limitations included in your vision of the business.

Goals and Milestones

This is a synopsis of the plan that you can refer to whenever you wish.

Describe your one-year, two-year, and long-term objectives, as well as the financial results you expect in those years of operation. Please do this in clear, simple, brief prose suitable for framing and hanging on your office wall.

6

Demonstrate Financial Credibility: Money Still Makes the World Go 'Round

Gerry Young

It's not money that brings happiness. It's lots of money.

Russian proverb

This chapter, like the next chapter on twenty-first-century grammar, is in the middle of the book because it applies equally to plans and proposals. Business is about money: earning, spending, saving, and investing money. The more you know about financing, the more favorably you will be perceived by investors and customers alike. The value of adjunct professionals such as attorneys and accountants to your long-term business is incalculable. You should have such counselors and listen to them. This chapter is not a foundation for your CPA certificate, but it will help in every aspect of your business.

It's rare for an entrepreneur to be a financial professional. Entrepreneurs come from across the spectrum of interests and achievements. A former helicopter pilot founded Federal Express; a college dropout started Microsoft. The drive to be an entrepreneur builds in people of all skills and all ages.

Let's assume you have what you're sure is a good business idea, but your knowledge of finance and accounting is limited. You certainly don't need to be a CPA or financial professional to succeed in business—some people, without a touch of irony, would even say it's a handicap. However, you do need to know at least enough about finance to:

- Raise the money you need to start your business and keep it running.
- Manage your business properly.

And (perhaps most importantly while you're trying to get funding):

- Convince potential investors or lenders that you know enough about finance to make the correct decisions as your business grows and prospers.

You'll probably need cash—maybe lots of it—to get your business up and running. Most likely you're going to need more than you can come up with from savings or other personal sources. To succeed at raising this cash, you're going to have to learn enough about finance and its particular language to inspire confidence among potential investors that you understand and are able to apply key financial principles.

This chapter covers the following topics:

1. Establishing Your Financing Requirements. This will cover the key steps in determining how much funding you will need.
2. Deciding What Type of Financing Your Company Should Seek. Should it be straight debt, equity in your company, or convertible securities (debt that can be converted to equity)?
3. Determining How These Funds Should Be Paid Back.
4. Constructing Your Financial Forecast. A well-thought-out and detailed multi-year forecast will be required to obtain any substantial funding. This is perhaps the most difficult, but important, section of this chapter.
5. Using Financial Ratios. These will be used by your potential lenders or investors to help them analyze your business plan. Appendix A discusses these ratios and how to calculate them, and recommends including the calculated ratios in your business plan.
6. Understanding Important Financial Terms. You want to make sure you can intelligently answer questions your potential investors and lenders may ask. Some of these will involve financial terms that you may not be familiar with. Many of them are explained and discussed throughout the chapter. Appendix C contains definitions of key financial expressions and concepts.
7. Educating Yourself. Finally, Appendix D shows some examples of websites that offer more advice or detail on specific types of topics related to the financial aspects of your business plan.

Let's focus on the nuts and bolts of putting together your financial forecast. This forecast will be an extremely important part of the package you present to potential lenders or investors. The initial parts of the chapter will explain some of the key financial concepts that relate to this forecast, starting with the legal form of the company you want to fund and moving on through the various types of funding you might consider getting and the differences among them, so you can understand the kind of funding—debt, equity, or a combination of both—that would suit your business best.

Let's examine your financing requirements one at a time.

HOW MUCH MONEY DO I NEED?

You can't answer this question without a solid financial forecast that predicts your profitability and your cash flow. One of the fundamental concepts you need to understand is that being profitable and having good cash flow are definitely NOT the same thing.[1] Without a good financial model, you won't be able to identify your real cash needs.

Once you have that forecast, it's vital to make sure you're asking for enough funding to get you through at least the first two years, even under pessimistic assumptions for revenue and profitability. Data on business failure in the United States show that if your business can survive these first few years, your odds of becoming a long-term success are much higher.

What Type of Company Are You?

Before you get too far into setting up your business plan, you should be sure that the type (or "form") of your company is the right one for your future needs. Your financial forecast content and layout will also depend to some extent on what the "form" of your business is. For example, some forms of business aren't themselves subject to income tax, while others are. The degree to which the compensation of the owner or owners is reflected in the company's financial statements will also depend on the form of business. Keep in mind that there are also non-financial considerations that will influence your choice on what the proper business form is for your situation.

The possible forms for a "for profit" business include a sole proprietorship, a partnership, a limited partnership, a regular ("C") corporation, an S corporation, or a limited liability company. All of these have their pluses and minuses. Let's look at each one briefly. Before choosing the form of your business, make sure you've had the advice of an attorney who specializes in these matters. Even if you already have your business established, you might need to revisit this topic to make sure you're organized in the best form for raising the financing you need.

Sole Proprietorship

This represents an individual doing business under an assumed business name. It's simple to set up, but offers limited opportunities for major expansion unless the form of the business is changed. This limitation exists because, without changing to a different form, the owner can't bring in partners and can't sell stock. The owner includes the profit or loss from the business in the personal income tax return, and has unlimited personal liability for whatever the company does, including all its debts.

Partnership

Legally, this is much the same as a sole proprietorship, except that there are several owners sharing the costs, profits, and liability. A formal partnership agreement is necessary for this form of business.

Limited Partnership

A limited partnership allows a number of investors who are shielded from much of the liability, but share in the profits. These are popular for ventures such as real estate investments. A "general partner" usually assumes most of the liability and may take a salary, while the limited partners do not usually draw a salary.

Corporation (C Corporation or S Corporation)

A corporation is really a legal "person" for many purposes. The owners (stockholders) may or may not be involved in management. In a C corporation (the form of most large businesses in the United States), the stockholders aren't taxed directly on the corporation's profits. Their tax liability would come on receiving cash dividend payments from the corporation or from selling their shares at a profit. In an S corporation, the owners are directly liable for income taxes on their share of the company's profits, but have limited liability in all other matters.[2]

Limited Liability Company

The LLC is a popular form of business. It behaves much like a corporation, and offers many of the same advantages. It has advantages that usually make it a better choice than a sole proprietorship, particularly because of the limitation of personal liability. You should consult an attorney in your state for specifics on how an LLC needs to be organized.[3]

One way to look at the differences among these business forms is to see how each one relates to three fundamental considerations:

- How many owners can there be?
- How much liability do the owners of the company accept?
- Are the owners of the business taxed on its profits directly?

Table 6.1 shows what the general rules are regarding these three considerations for each type of organization. You can see, for example, that in the

Table 6.1
Three Essential Considerations of Each Form of Business

	# of Owners	Owner Liability	Owner Taxed on Company Profits?
Sole Proprietorship	1	Unlimited	Yes
Partnership	Many	Unlimited	Yes
Limited Partnership	Many	Limited, except for the general partner	Depends on partnership agreement
C Corporation	Many	Limited	No
S Corporation	Many	Limited	Yes
LLC (Limited Liability Company)	Depends on state laws	Limited	Yes

case of a sole proprietorship (one owner) or a partnership (a number of owners), each owner assumes unlimited liability for the company's debts and actions, and is taxed on his or her share of the company's profits.

Before you make the decision as to how to form your business (or change the way your existing business is legally organized) you'll need the advice of a good general business attorney.

When you've decided on the form of your business operation, you'll still have to file the proper documents with your state, including registering a business name.

You must register your business name before you start using it. The name may not reasonably be confused with a pre-existing business. You couldn't, for example, start a new bank and call it "Chase Manhattan" or "Bank of America." Your state may have a website that allows you to browse names to see if someone else is already using the name you've thought of. The name isn't official until it has been registered.

You'll have to comply with some other formalities, especially if you plan to have employees. See Appendix D for the IRS website address, which outlines many of these requirements.

Once all this has been done, you're "official," and can approach lenders or investors to raise funds.

HOW TO USE YOUR FINANICAL FORECAST TO ESTIMATE FUNDING NEEDS

A separate section of this chapter discusses the financial forecast in quite a bit of detail. Let's assume that your forecast is finished. You have created a detailed forecast of your revenue, profitability, and cash flow on a month-by-month basis for (let's say) a three-year period. We'll also assume that you've been over this several times to modify the assumptions and make sure they're reasonable and that you've checked the results to make sure they're reasonable. To gain financing, they should also be "conservative." This term, used when referring to financial forecasts, has nothing to do with politics. It means that you've been somewhat modest—underestimating revenue and overestimating costs, for example—so that potential lenders and investors will have more confidence you can achieve the predicted results.

If you're starting a new business and are like most start-ups, your cash flow will be negative at the beginning of your operation. You'll probably have some significant expenses in getting your company established and you likely won't have much revenue yet, as it takes a while to build up a good customer base. Your plan, to be appealing to investors, should show steady growth in customers and, eventually, in profitability and cash flow. It must be able to withstand scrutiny by experienced (and skeptical) professionals.

If you're an established business with several years of operating history, there are obviously a wide range of possible historic results that you've already achieved, ranging from severe financial problems to substantial growth in revenues, profitability, and cash flow. This history can be helpful in putting together your financial forecast.

Whether you've based your results on some period of actual operations or are forecasting a brand-new business, let's assume you're now holding the result of all the work. It will show you your revenues, profits, cash flow (and many other details) for each month of a multi-year period.

First, take your forecast and, as described below, put in pessimistic assumptions regarding your revenue, profitability and, most important, cash flow. Take out any assumptions you've put in regarding adding debt or equity financing (just change the amounts to zero on your Assumptions tab). Now, as a rough initial estimate of your cash needs, look at the highest *negative* cash balance over the life of the forecast. This is the minimum you'll need. In fact, you'll need more than this amount. You must make sure you're asking for enough money—it's easier to get more money at the beginning than to have to go "back to the well" and ask for more later on.

Why will you need more than the minimum? The best reason is that, no matter how much time you've put into your forecast, there's one sure thing you know about it—it'll be wrong. It may be too pessimistic or, more likely, it'll be too optimistic. Count on it being wrong.

You'll need more than the minimum just to allow for uncertainty and for the likelihood you've been a bit optimistic in how fast you'll gain customers and in how low your operating costs will be. As any experienced traveler can tell you on the eve of your next vacation, bring half the clothing and twice the money you think you'll need.

Now we're ready to move on to deciding what type of funding to try for.

WHAT TYPE OF FINANCING SHOULD YOU SEEK?

Your main choices in financing are:

- A business loan, which can be secured[4] or unsecured. This could come from a bank or other financial institution as a normal loan or as an SBA[5] guaranteed loan. It could also come from an individual or venture capital firm that specializes in supporting enterprises in your industry. It could even come from another company, perhaps a potential supplier or customer.
- A convertible debt instrument, which behaves like a loan, but can allow the investor to convert the loan into equity (ownership) in the company at some time in the future.
- A straight equity investment.

Commercial Loans

A bank[6] loan is usually one of the first alternatives that people think of, and it can be a good choice. However, banks aren't in the business of "investing" in companies—they're in the business of making good loans. To a banker, a "good" loan is a safe loan. That means a loan that's well secured or is made to someone who has substantial financial resources (compared to the amount of the loan) and an excellent credit rating.

It's possible to get a substantial unsecured loan from a bank, but you should assume that you're going to have to come up with enough collateral to, in effect, "guarantee" the loan.[7] Your business, if it's already up and running, may have its own collateral in the form of accounts receivable, inventory, fixed assets such as machinery or equipment, or real estate. If your business doesn't have sufficient assets, the bank will want you to pledge personal assets. Besides establishing good collateral, this also shows that you believe in your business idea strongly enough to risk your house, cars, or other valuable possessions.

A couple of points to keep in mind before approaching a bank or other financial institution:

- Banks are not interested in acquiring ownership interests in companies. They want good loans in their portfolio and a good "depository relationship."[8]
- You needn't confine yourself to "regular" banks that offer checking and savings accounts, advertise on billboards, etc. There are a number of specialized financial companies who focus on lending small businesses money. Many of them focus on asset-based lending, and will only loan money that's backed by accounts receivable, inventory, or other assets of the firm.
- Finally, you should understand that almost any loan you obtain will require regular monthly payments. The interest and principal payments associated with these should be built into your financial plan before you show it to a bank.

Equity

At the other end of the scale from raising money through loans is selling equity, or ownership in the business. You can't just go around informally selling ownership in the business without first getting some advice from a business attorney. State or federal securities laws may impose requirements that you'll absolutely need to follow. There are potentially heavy penalties for violations in this area, so pick your advisers with care.

The key factor in understanding prospective equity investors is that equity is riskier than debt. Debt is generally secured with some sort of collateral, and in the ugly event of bankruptcy a lender has a decent chance of recovering some or all of the balance; equity investors are generally facing a loss of their entire investment.

The most famous (and notorious) source of equity is a venture capital (VC) firm. If you fit their model, these companies can be good sources of financing. However, they generally look for companies who offer extremely high growth potential and outstanding returns on investment.[9] Discussing VCs in depth is outside the scope of this chapter, but learning more about them is fairly easy. There are many books available, or, if you want to research this on your own, just go to your Internet browser, type in "venture capital presentations," and prepare to read through a lot of material. This should give you a good orientation toward these types of companies.

If you don't meet the extreme growth and profit potential that the VC people usually demand, you might look for what's known as "angel investors" in your area. These are typically people of high net worth who are interested in helping local businesses. Your banker, attorney, or CPA should have leads to angel investors who might be interested in talking to you.

Equity Investors vs. Lenders

Before you talk to anyone about equity investments, you need to understand that equity investors have much different expectations than do lenders. This is only fair—someone who chooses a riskier investment would rationally have to demand a higher return than from a safer one—otherwise, the safer alternative at the same return would always be chosen. This would be like someone offering you two choices—you can buy a certain product for $10 with a thirty-year absolute guarantee, or $10 without the guarantee. You'd obviously take the offer with the guarantee. In order for you to accept the risk of going without the guarantee, you have to get a better price deal.

Therefore, equity holders will insist on getting a higher return on their investment than if they'd just loaned the money. This relates to a financial concept called the "security market line" or, more plainly, the "risk/reward tradeoff." Figure 6.1 illustrates the concept.

Figure 6.1
The Security Market Line

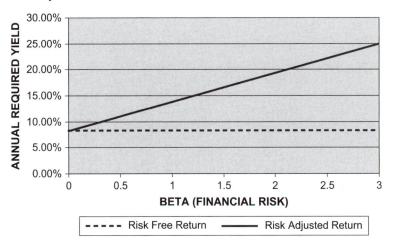

This is really quite simple: The higher the degree of risk the investor accepts, the higher the return the investor will demand. From a common-sense standpoint, this is easily understandable—anyone would want to get "paid" somehow for risking money in an investment, and the more the risk, the more the payment should be.

You can see in our example chart that a zero-risk investment has an expected return of about 8 percent. The beta (risk) scale goes from zero to a fairly high risk. Way out on the right-hand side, you can see that for a risky investment an investor might expect an annual return of 25 percent or more risk—much more in the cases of VC firms. A VC who expects to get 10 times the investment back in five years is asking for an annual return of over 58 percent. The return (the vertical axis on the left) is always some amount greater than zero. The beta for a company that isn't publicly traded can't easily be determined, but investors will probably regard it as being a number significantly greater than the 1.0 that represents an average publicly traded firm. This is because of the risks and uncertainty[10] usually associated with smaller high-growth ventures.

The interest rate a bank charges may be, as of this writing, from 8 percent to perhaps 12 percent on commercial loans. Equity investors would never accept an expected return that low. If that was all they expected to get, they'd loan the money instead and get the additional security that a loan offers. If you want investors to give up the relative safety of a loan and move to equity, you have to "pay" them to do it. The way you pay is to show that they will get a much higher return by owning part of the company.

Finally, major equity investors may insist on having a voice in the day-to-day running of the business. An investor willing to put substantial funds into the company may insist on a certain number of seats on the board of directors or perhaps the right to name some high-level officers of the company, such as the chief operating or chief financial officer.

Convertible Debt

In between equity and debt (loans) is what is called "convertible debt." There's a wide variety of these, because financial people just love to invent new kinds of securities and financial instruments. But they all come down to one thing: They start out life as a debt instrument, behaving just like a loan. However, at some point they can be converted to a certain amount of equity. This makes them attractive to venture capitalists, among others.

They're attractive because a debt instrument offers better security to the lender/investor. It is often, if not usually, collateralized.[11] Even when it's not, lenders can often recover substantial funds if a firm goes bankrupt, while those who hold equity usually end up with zero. At some point, however, it might be more profitable to the investor to convert it to equity.

You can see why the VC people like this type of investment. They get to have it both ways—the security of a collateralized loan at the beginning, and the higher returns of equity later on.

As you've probably already guessed, you will need both legal and financial professionals to set up a convertible instrument.

PAYING BACK YOUR FINANCIERS

If your financing came through a pure debt instrument, such as a commercial loan, the payback is virtually automatic. You'll be required to make regular monthly payments that include both principal on the loan and the interest payments.

If you sold convertible debt, you'll have a similar situation, where you'll have to pay interest (or dividend) on the debt until it's converted to equity.

However, equity is a little bit trickier to pay back. Let's discuss this briefly. You'll need to be familiar with this topic in the event you're talking to potential equity investors.

Paying Back Equity Investors

This brings us to a concept you'll have to understand if you're going to offer equity or a convertible instrument: "exit strategy." This is financial-speak for "how do I get cash out of the company if I hold equity?" As you can understand, just owning equity in the company doesn't mean that the investor can actually realize a profit on the original investment. Unless your company becomes publicly traded, allowing anyone to buy or sell its stock, there might not be an easy way for these investors to cash out and get the return they hoped for.

It may not be realistic to promise that they should count on ending up with publicly traded stock. "Going public," as the process of offering stock to the public for the first time is called, is complex, expensive, and risky.[12] However, there are other alternatives. For example, if your company is doing well, you'll find it easier to raise debt from banks and other lending institutions. If this is the case, you'd be able to "buy out" your equity investors by borrowing money and cashing them out.

Ideally, the company should be able to take the initiative in buying out these investors. The original investment agreement might specify either a promised annual rate of return—a risky promise to make—or, more prudently, tie the increase to the "book value per share"[13] at the time the investment is made and the time when it's liquidated. It's best for the company if the company determines when to buy out the investors, although this will obviously make the investment a harder sell.

Remember our "security market line" concept? When you're planning to buy out these equity investors, keep in mind that a savvy equity investor will expect, and probably demand, double-digit returns. This means that he'll expect annual gains from his investment of at least 10 percent (and probably much more). These gains can mount up in a hurry.

For example, an investor who put in $150,000 at the beginning and was cashed out five years later would get over $300,000 if her annual return was

15 percent. If the annual return was 20 percent, she'd get more than $370,000. A few percentage points can make a huge difference. However, without these types of investors, you wouldn't have become the successful entrepreneur you are at the five-year mark, so give the money with a big smile and sincere thanks for the help.

This brings us to explaining how to put together the type of financial forecast that's expected by bankers, venture capitalists, or experienced private investors. Without a solid financial forecast, you'll have little chance of getting significant funding.

THE FINANCIAL FORECAST

Your Responsibilities

It's fairly easy to find financial professionals who can put together a good business forecast for you, probably by using software like Microsoft Excel. Many, but certainly not all, certified public accountants may be able to do this. Businesses and consultants experienced in financial analysis and business planning should be able to do it. Your bank or your attorney may be able to refer experts in this field. You should interview candidates for this key job thoroughly. They should be able to provide references of firms for which they've done similar work.

Many of these experts would be glad to do the whole job, including making up the assumptions that really drive the plan. But you should resist delegating entirely the financial considerations of your start-up. It's your job as the entrepreneur to put in some serious time thinking about the economics of your business and coming up with these key assumptions. Once you've figured out the answers to some of the questions below, you can then hand over the assumptions to a professional to turn them into a financial forecast. (This may also save you some money on consulting time, but your primary concern here is to get the best plan possible, and that means it has to rely heavily on your knowledge and intuition as to how your business will perform in the future.)

Be prepared—this part of your business plan task will take a lot of serious thinking on your part, and probably some research into the economics of your business and your industry. Luckily, this research, thanks to all the data on the World Wide Web, is now a lot easier and quicker than it used to be.

Gathering Financial Information

If your business is already established, you'll have some historical financial statements that can be used as a foundation for putting together this forecast. You'll also have an idea on some of the key assumptions that need to be made. Table 6.2 shows a sample of the kinds of information that are needed to put together a good financial forecast. This is not a complete list; some of the items on it may not apply to your type of business.

Table 6.2
Essential Elements of a Hard-Working Financial Forecast

Customers/Revenue and Direct Cost	Overhead Expenses	Balance Sheet/Cash Flow
New customers gained per month	Staff headcount required in each functional area	Average days of receivables
Average revenue per customer	Salary for each position	Average days of payables
Customers lost per month	Payroll tax and benefit cost for each position	Average days of inventory
Products/services sold to each customer	Building rent	Fixed assets[a] required for operation of the business
Variable cost[b] of each product or service	Marketing, sales and advertising costs	Depreciable lives of each asset type
Bad debt[c] allowance	Utility costs Communications costs Travel and entertainment expense	Loan repayment schedules

[a]A "fixed asset," in financial terms, refers to real estate or equipment used in the operation of the business. Usually a minimum threshold is set (such as $2,000) and a requirement that items to be capitalized have a useful life measured in years rather than days or a few months. Items costing less than this are treated as an expense, but if they cost more than that, they're carried on your financial statements as a "fixed asset." These are assets that usually depreciate over time, meaning that you recognize as a monthly expense only a percentage of the original cost until that cost is all used up, making the asset "fully depreciated."

[b]"Variable cost" means all the costs that are directly associated with providing a unit of product or service. This will be discussed, with examples, in more detail later in this chapter and in Addendum 2.

[c]It's unfortunately true that you'll probably have customers who don't pay 100% of what they owe you. You should set aside an estimated amount each month for possible bad debt losses. This is also discussed more later in this chapter.

Thinking Monthly

Always start your forecasts at the lowest practical detail level in terms of time; this is the monthly level, rather than quarterly or annual. You can always roll a monthly forecast up into quarterly and annual totals, but you can't easily break down a forecast that's built on annual assumptions into separate months. It really isn't practical to do a forecast based on time periods less than a month, so we'll start with that level of time detail.

Why worry about doing this on a monthly rather than an annual basis?

- First, this will make you think about your business somewhat more deeply, rather than making gross assumptions about a whole year.
- Second, it'll show variations in key factors such as cash flow that may not be visible on a total year.

- Third, your potential lenders or investors will probably expect it—that's the best reason of all.

Revenue and Its "Buckets"

Revenue (or "Sales") is by far the most important part of your forecasting process. Many of your other financial figures will depend partially or entirely on your revenue forecast. Clearly your direct (variable) costs will depend on revenue. But when you think about it, you can also see that your overhead staffing and other costs that may seem fixed[14] will eventually have to rise and fall with revenue as will many of your other line items.

There are many ways to do sales forecasting. The bad news is that none of these is really scientific, and none will produce completely accurate results. If you search for "sales forecasting" on the Web, you'll see lots of sites that offer advice on how to do this by estimating market share, or using similar high-level techniques. The market-share technique, which I've seen used with disastrous results, first estimates the size of the market you're competing in. This could be as small as the market for boutique decorators in a rural area, or as large as electronic companies in the United States. Then you simply assume that you'll get a certain share of the market—for example, 3.5 percent—and there's your forecast! The problem is that the people who may buy your product don't know that you're supposed to get 3.5 percent of their business, so they may not buy from you at all. In your Web search, you'll also find a number of people eager to sell you fancy statistical models based on projecting new sales based on past trends.[15] These might even work until there's a change in your competition, your own products, or the economy. These changes tend to happen with distressing regularity.

If these high-level methods don't work for you—and they probably won't—what should you do?

The best way to estimate your revenue is first to separate it into categories, or "buckets" that describe your main lines of business. Then, as you'll see in the section below, we'll use the "input-output" method to develop an actual forecast. For example, in a retail clothing store, you might set up separate buckets for men's and women's clothing, or even separate those into subcategories. If you're running an advertising agency, you might set up separate buckets by client type—manufacturing, retail, service companies, etc. The point is to go into enough detail to show meaningful breakdowns to the lenders and investors and, more importantly, to give you ongoing information about how your revenue is progressing against your forecast in each category. This will help you identify problems and take action to make your business more successful.

To an outside observer, these buckets will make it clear that you've put in some serious thought about the main driving factors of your business. For you, the separate buckets will provide a much better handle on your business's behavior than a single revenue figure. This detail will give you much better insight into how your revenue is meeting expectations than a single figure will.

I hope you are persuaded that a single line called Revenue in your business plan doesn't give you the information you need—or that potential lenders or investors expect—to track and manage your business. Now let's talk about how you can actually forecast revenue for each of the buckets you've decided on.

One cautionary note: Before you dig into the details below, please take this one piece of advice—bring your sales and marketing people into the forecasting process. You don't have to take their word as gospel, but their input can be valuable. More importantly, your forecast becomes their target for achievement in the coming years, and therefore is a big part of their expected compensation. If they don't buy into it, you'll face some major problems in the coming months.

Practical Forecasting: The Input-Output Method

To forecast your revenue, you'll have to devise a method of forecasting based on all the different sales channels that your company uses.

Let's start with some examples of sales channels that a business can use to gain revenue and customers:

- Advertising (outdoor displays, Yellow Pages ads, radio/TV ads, etc.)
- Direct mail
- Telemarketing
- Catalog distribution
- Outside salespeople calling on customers personally
- Inside salespeople phoning targeted customers
- Website sales
- Inbound call centers to take orders

If you're a retail business, you'll also get a lot of sales from people just coming to your store ("foot traffic"). Part of this traffic may be a result of advertising, direct mail, or other methods, but some will probably just be people who needed a particular product and found your business.

For anything other than this casual traffic, you can use the input-output method of forecasting sales. In this method, your "inputs" are the quantitative factors related to your direct mail campaign, your salespeople calling on customers, the hits on your website, and so on. The "output" of this effort and expenditure is a certain number of customers buying a certain number of items or a specific dollar amount. Let's look at two examples to show you how to quantify the inputs and the outputs to come up with a forecast.

Direct Mail

In direct mail, you send out a large number of items to a targeted list of commercial or residential customers. Let's say you send out 100,000 pieces of direct mail advertising either your business in general or some particular items that you think will appeal to your target audience. You plan on mailing three times in the coming year: in March, July and October.

In direct mail, the response rate is usually quite low, somewhere in the low single-digit percent range. For our example, let's say you expect a 1.5 percent positive response, and that each person responding will place an order for $75 of merchandise. Let's also say that these sales will happen one month after your mailing.

Now for your output, based on these assumptions: Your revenue forecast would show 1,500 responses at $75 each, for total revenue of $112,500 in each of the months of April, August and November.

Outside Salespeople

Companies with outside salespeople calling on customers usually have a pretty good idea of the "productivity" of each salesperson. For example, you might have two different types of salespeople—one type (the more experienced) calling on existing customers to build the volume they order and cold-calling on potential large accounts, and the other type cold-calling on smaller accounts. Let's assume that the first type of salesperson might produce average revenue per month of $30,000 and the second type $15,000 per month. In the first case, you might plan on calling on fifty customers a month, and "closing the sale" on 20 percent of them, with an average buy per customer of $3,000. Similar numbers could go into the second type of salesperson. These factors make up your "input" assumptions.

If you now have three of the first type of salesperson and ten of the second, you'd forecast $90,000 of revenue per month from your higher-level people and $150,000 per month from the lower-level people. This would give you total sales per month of $240,000. This is the "output" result of your assumptions.

Why go to the trouble of using a method like this, instead of just looking at historical results and trending them? Because this technique forces you to understand—and quantify—the factors that drive your revenue. It will also, more importantly, give you a way to go back later and find out exactly why your forecast was wrong (which it definitely will be).

To analyze what causes variances between your forecast and what was actually achieved, you have to dig into the numbers and see how actual performance compared to what you assumed. If, instead of using input-output calculations, you'd just chosen a dollar number for new sales in each month, you'd have no way to analyze what went wrong (or for what went better than expected—let's stay optimistic here!).

In the salesperson example, you can track each salesperson's activity. You might find that one salesperson appeared to fall short mainly because he hadn't called on enough potential customers; another because of a low close rate; but the third, despite falling a little short in revenue per sale, exceeded expectations in her close rate and in number of potential customers called on. In each of these cases, the remedial action is obvious—more calls, better closing technique training, and training in up-selling to get a higher revenue per sale, respectively. If you hadn't used input-output, you'd have no concrete idea of why each salesperson's results varied from the forecast, or what could be done to improve results.

In the direct mail example, you can track response rates and average amounts purchased to see where the variances are and in which direction. If you found a low response rate, for example, one possibility would be better culling of your direct mail list and another might be to search out another source of prospect addresses.

In both cases, the variance details revealed by the input-output method help you identify what action to take and how to change your assumptions to make them more realistic.

Taking Seasonality into Account

Many businesses—perhaps most—have seasonal peaks and valleys in their revenue. For example, retailers usually expect November and December to be peak months because of Christmas shopping. Other firms, especially "B to B" companies (businesses focusing on sales to other businesses) may see seasonal downturns in these same months because they depend on people being in their offices to make purchasing decisions. Hotels and other leisure-related businesses may see peaks in volume during the spring and summer, while others may see lower volumes because their buyers are off on vacation.

If these factors may apply to your business, you should take this into account in your forecasts. This is most easily done by first ignoring the seasonality factor. Use your input-output assumptions without any regard for seasonality, to get a baseline forecast. This is called a "normalized" forecast.

Next, for each of your revenue buckets, estimate a seasonality factor for each month of the year. A month that's going to be exactly "average" would have a factor of 1.000. If you're a retailer and expect great sales in December, your December seasonality factor might be high—perhaps 1.800 or higher. If summer is a downtime, you may have factors like 0.750 or 0.600. Pick round numbers if you have no history to go on.

You should also take the number of business days in each month into account. All things being equal, a month with twenty-two business days (days excluding weekends and holidays[16]) will give you better sales volume than one with nineteen business days. Accounting for the number of days you're open for business is especially important for businesses that deal on a retail basis; there are just more days for people to buy things from you.

Key point: The factors for all twelve months must add up to 12.000. Keep adjusting until this is true. If you use factors that add up to more than 12.000, you'll be overstating your revenue. If they add up to less, your revenue will be understated. Don't worry about being exact—just putting in rough estimates will be a big help in making your forecast more realistic. As you accumulate operating history, you can improve your estimates.

To produce your final monthly forecast, just multiply the monthly normalized revenue forecast by that month's seasonality factor. Table 6.3 shows what it might look like on a spreadsheet.

You can see that the total calendar year revenue forecast for this revenue bucket is higher than the normalized forecast. This can happen in either direction; in fact, it'd be a wild coincidence if the normalized and seasonalized revenues came out to be the same. In this case, the main reason the adjusted forecast is higher is because of the high seasonality factor for December. Figure 6.2 shows what the results look like on a graph.

This same process can be repeated for each of your revenue buckets (commercial versus residential, western versus eastern regions, etc.). It's possible that you'd have different seasonality factors for different buckets, so keep your mind open to how you think things will really behave.

Direct Costs

Once you have your revenue forecast set up properly, you need to start considering how to estimate your direct costs. "Direct" or "variable" costs are the costs that you incur to produce a product or service. Another way to think about it is that "direct" costs are the costs that change in the short run as your revenue goes up (or down, although we won't dwell on this possibility too much). This part will also take some serious thinking.

Bad Debt

The first category of direct cost you put in is your estimate of bad debt losses for each revenue bucket. It's a common accounting practice to lump this expense into your overhead expenses (also referred to as "Operating" or "Sales, General and Administrative" expenses, but this is a case where common practice is not the best practice). The reason for this is that bad debt obviously varies with your level of revenue—the more you sell, the higher your potential bad debt losses must be.[17] Putting the bad debt in as a direct cost gives you a more realistic look at your net revenue, or the revenue that's left after accounting for bad debt.

Standard accounting rules (known as GAAP for Generally Accepted Accounting Principles) dictate that you can't "recognize" revenue (that is, you can't book it on your financial statements) unless it's "realizable." This means that it has to be almost certain that payment will be received and retained in a form that has value. Therefore, the net revenue is really just the GAAP revenue that accountants measure.

It's best to be conservatively high in estimating your bad debt, especially if you're starting a new business. While trying to get your business up and running, you'll find it difficult to turn down business; this may lead to higher than normal bad debt expenses.[18]

Table 6.3
Monthly Forecast Spreadsheet

	January	February	March	April	May	June	July	August	September	October	November	December	TOTAL
Normalized Forecast	$15,000	$15,375	$15,759	$16,153	$16,557	$16,971	$17,395	$17,830	$18,276	$18,733	$19,201	$19,681	**$206,933**
Seasonality Factor	0.975	0.950	1.015	1.000	1.030	0.950	0.850	0.875	1.050	1.150	0.905	1.250	
Seasonality Total	12.000												
Monthly Forecast	$14,625	$14,606	$15,996	$16,153	$17,054	$16,123	$14,786	$15,602	$19,190	$21,543	$17,377	$24,602	**$207,656**

Figure 6.2
Normalized vs. Seasonalized Forecast

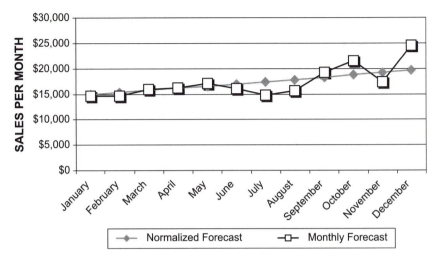

A simple way to estimate your bad debt is to have your accountant pre-pare for you each month a report called a Detailed Aged Accounts Receiva-ble. This will list all your customers and show how much they owe by thrity-day categories. Anything that they've owed for less than thirty days is called Current, with the next columns being 30–60 days, 60–90 days, and over 90 days. Based on your experience with your customers, you might decide to reserve all amounts over ninety days and half of the dollars in the sixty-day bucket. If you have customers who always pay, but pay late, you can exclude all or part of their debts to you from this calculation.[19]

If you're in retail or another type of business that doesn't extend trade credit, but has customers who always pay by credit card, your bad debt estimate can be minimal (but not zero, as customers who complain can often get their credit charges reversed). In these cases you should deduct the credit card company's fees from your revenue as a direct cost.

Other Direct Costs

Here's where you're going to have to do some real thinking about the costs involved with producing each of your products or services. These will vary depending on the type of business you're in. If you run a retail store, some of the obvious direct costs are the cost of buying your product from the manufacturer, shipping costs, and sales or other direct taxes. But if your sales staff works on commission, their commission costs (and the associated payroll taxes) are probably also variable with the amount actually sold. Here are some recommendations on how you might approach doing this in a thorough and thoughtful way:

- Get your people together in a brainstorming session for a few hours and talk about what costs you'll incur for each type of product or service you offer. In a session like this, you want to encourage people to come up with all kinds of ideas. Later on, you can all filter these down to a better list. You may introduce this by explaining that what you're concerned about is identifying all the costs that are directly tied to each product or service. You're not concerned with allocating costs that don't vary directly.
- If you're already established as a business, pull all your accounts payable invoices (amounts you owe to the various suppliers and vendors) and sift these into three piles: definite direct costs, definite fixed or overhead costs, and those that are "in between" (they might vary somewhat with your production, but also have portions that tend to stay fixed). Think about what would happen to each amount if, for example, your revenue doubled.
- Be careful not to go overboard in imputing what are really overhead costs as direct costs. For example, sales commissions, if they're paid as a percent of revenue, are variable costs, but the base salary of your salespeople is fixed.

To see some additional hints and examples on how to go about computing these direct cost factors, please see Appendix B.

The point here is to be open-minded and creative about figuring out what all the direct costs are for a given product or service you sell. Knowing that, you'll know your margin,[20] or the percent of revenue that actually contributes to covering your operating costs and producing a profit.

A smart business leader concentrates on managing to maximize total margin, rather than revenue. This can't be done effectively without accurate and complete estimates of your direct costs.

Operating Costs

Whether you call these "operating costs" or "SG&A" (Sales, General and Administrative), these are the costs that do not vary directly and immediately with your revenue. The salaries and benefits of your employees, your building rent and utilities, and similar expenses all go into this category.

One trap that an unwary or inexperienced business owner might fall into when analyzing or forecasting these costs is to assume that they're "fixed," meaning that they don't vary at all with revenue. Even though they don't vary directly like the variable costs you analyzed so carefully in our previous step, they will vary in the long run.[21] If your business grows substantially, you'll need more staff, perhaps a larger building, higher budgets for travel, advertising, telecommunications, business insurance, and so on. A savvy reader of your plan will quickly notice if your operating costs stay relatively flat.

One simple modeling technique to handle this is to establish a starting dollar level for each operating cost category and to set a percent rate at which the category will increase with revenue. The better, but more time-consuming way, is to set up rules as to how each category will change as your business grows. For example, you might say that rent will stay the same until you hit a certain revenue threshold, at which time you'll need a new building to accommodate all your employees, and then will jump to a higher level.

Staffing Costs

Let's start by looking at how you forecast the biggest category of operating costs for most businesses—the wage-related costs of your employees. Probably the easiest way to do this is to start with a "headcount" forecast. List all the departments in your company. Your list might look something like this:

- Executive Management
- Sales and Marketing
- Operations/Production
- Finance
- Information Technology
- Human Resources

For each of these departments, list the current employees by title. These people will either be salaried or hourly. The senior people may have incentive compensations that pay a bonus if the company hits certain targets. The salespeople probably have at least part of their pay dependent on commissions. I suggest building a table that looks something like Table 6.4. The figures are used for example purposes only—you'll have to build in the costs particular to your business.

You can see that this takes account of all the compensation-related costs of each employee. Some (the hourly staff) may have overtime pay. Others, particularly those in the sales organization, will earn commissions.[22] Selected employees may be eligible for incentive compensation that will depend on the company achieving certain revenue or profitability targets.

Benefit costs, in our example sheet, cost the same amount per employee per month. Some companies may offer different levels of benefits to different classes of employees, but this feature can be added easily. Notice that the payroll taxes that the company must pay for each employee are calculated as a percent of salary,[23] as are the overtime, commissions and incentive compensation. Different companies may modify these based on their own experience—the point is to include all these categories to make sure you're capturing the real total compensation cost per employee, which is significantly higher than the nominal salary or wage.

This example may be too simple for some companies, but it's easily customizable. You can—and should—customize this to suit your own company's cost structure. It can also accommodate new employees you'll want to add during the forecast period.

Table 6.4
Effective Method for Forecasting Employee Compensation

| Benefit Cost/Employee | $350.00 per month | | | | | | | | | |
| Payroll Taxes | 13.50% of gross pay | | | | | Medical insurance contribution by company Company-paid portion | | | | |

Job Title	Salary or Hourly	Base Pay	Overtime	Comm.	Incentive	Gross Annual Pay w/o Benefits	Payroll Taxes	Annual Benefit Cost	Total Annual Comp Cost	Average Monthly Cost
EXECUTIVE MANAGEMENT										
President/CEO	Salary	$110,000.00			20.00%	$132,000.00	$17,820.00	$4,200.00	$154,020.00	$12,835.00
Administrative Assistant	Hourly	$41,600.00	10.00%			$47,840.00	$6,458.40	$4,200.00	$58,498.40	$4,874.87
SALES AND MARKETING										
VP, Sales & Marketing	Salary	$85,000.00			10.00%	$93,500.00	$12,622.50	$4,200.00	$110,322.50	$9,193.54
Director of Sales	Salary	$75,000.00		5.00%		$78,750.00	$10,631.25	$4,200.00	$93,581.25	$7,798.44
Outside Sales Person #1	Salary	$55,000.00		25.00%		$68,750.00	$9,281.25	$4,200.00	$82,231.25	$6,852.60
Outside Sales Person #2	Salary	$52,000.00		25.00%		$65,000.00	$8,775.00	$4,200.00	$77,975.00	$6,497.92
Outside Sales Person #3	Salary	$48,000.00		25.00%		$60,000.00	$8,100.00	$4,200.00	$72,300.00	$6,025.00
Sales Commission Clerk	Hourly	$42,000.00	15.00%			$51,450.00	$6,945.75	$4,200.00	$62,595.75	$5,216.31

Other Operating Costs

Staffing costs are the most difficult to forecast, but you'll also have to put some time in looking at the other categories of operating costs. Keep a sharp eye on these to identify if, and how much, they might vary in the long run as your business grows. The categories here will include such items as:

- Leases or rent
- Utilities
- Advertising
- Telecommunications costs
- Insurance
- Travel and entertainment
- Outside services (legal, accounting, consulting)
- ... and probably other categories as well

For each of these, you'll have to come up with a starting level of monthly cost and some idea of how, if at all, they might change over time. Some of them, such as business insurance, may occur only a few times a year in relatively large amounts, while others, such as your office space rent, may not vary at all from month to month.

Breakeven: How Revenue, Direct Costs, and Operating Costs Tie Together

Before leaping into the topic of actually putting together the forecast, it may be helpful to discuss breakeven analysis. Like many financial concepts, this is fairly simple once you think about it for a while. This is also a topic that your potential lender or investor may ask you about, and it's always best to be prepared for that with a chart already set up.

Figure 6.3 is a simple breakeven chart—it shows how your operating ("fixed") and direct costs interact with your revenue growth to calculate a breakeven point, or a point where your operating income stops being negative and starts being positive (this is a good thing).

Your revenue is simple—it's just a line that grows from zero at the bottom left to wherever you think your maximum possible monthly revenue is. Your costs are the total of your operating costs and your direct costs. You can see in our example that the solid line (revenue) crosses the short dashed line (total costs = operating costs plus direct costs) at a certain point. The horizontal dashed line represents operating costs, to which the direct costs are added to come up with total costs. The point where the revenue line crosses the total cost line is the breakeven point. If your revenue is higher than that, you have positive operating income[24]; if it's less, you have negative operating income.

This chart is called a "simple" breakeven because it treats operating costs as totally fixed, whereas in reality they probably either slope upward

Figure 6.3
Simple Breakeven Chart (Start-up)

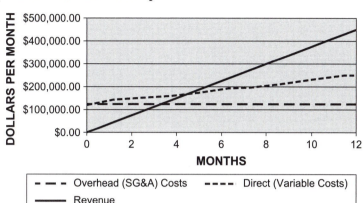

a bit or perhaps have a "step function," where they stay flat for a period and then jump to a higher level which stays flat for a while, and so on.

With the information you've put together so far, you can build a break-even chart by just building a table of all your revenue buckets and their corresponding direct cost buckets to come up with a blended average ratio of direct cost to revenue. This is the slope of the solid red line.

BUILDING YOUR FORECAST

Make sure the professional who puts the model together understands that the final version of the model will be delivered to you for your own use, rather than being retained at the expert's location. You don't want to be in the position of paying the outside expert every time you want to change assumptions or re-run the model.

Here are some recommendations on how to instruct this professional to do it, or, if you want to do it yourself, how you should build it to make it easier to use and document. A word of caution: Unless you have the following, you should farm this out to someone with experience in this area:

- Substantial experience in building forecasts and using spreadsheet programs.
- Thorough understanding of how asset, liability, equity, revenue and expense accounts relate to each other in the compilation of accounting statements.
- Lots of time to spend on this activity.

This is no place for a beginner to try to put together a first forecast.

Now let's talk about how to get a good start on this forecast, whether you're doing it yourself or farming it out to an expert. A little bit of prior planning can save you from the problems that result from a business plan model that's too complex to understand or change.

Your goal is to create a self-documenting model with external[25] assumptions, so it can be quickly changed without editing dozens (or hundreds) of formulas. A model built this way, with all the key assumptions consolidated onto a single tab, is not only simpler to change and maintain, but also gives you an easy way to show a potential lender or investor your key assumptions. If your financial model looks professional, you'll be building credibility with the potential funding sources who will examine it.

Pay attention to how this model is organized. Give explicit direction to the person who's doing it, so that it's self-documenting, is organized well, and will present a professional appearance.

If you try to cram too much onto a single spreadsheet tab, it'll become confusing and hard to figure out. Microsoft Excel and similar programs have the capability of creating a large number of "tabs" (separate pages within a single workbook). Use this capability to separate the model into specific parts that come together to produce the final forecast. This will make the model easier to understand and organize.

Following is an overview of suggested tabs.

Assumptions

This tab will contain all the numerical assumptions that drive your financial model. All other tabs will refer back to this tab to do their calculations. That way, the model's documentation will be easy to understand, with no hidden surprises in its formulas that can't be seen or easily changed. Using this method makes it easy to change the results of the various formulas by just changing the appropriate cell on the *Assumptions* tab.

This tab should have different sections for different types of assumptions. Typical sections on this tab might include:

- Sales/revenue growth[26] (separated by revenue buckets).
- Direct costs[27] (separated by revenue bucket).
- Headcount and staffing expenses.
- Other operating costs.
- Capital expenditures.
- Debt.
- Equity contributions.
- Balance sheet assumptions.[28]
- General economic assumptions, such as interest rates, tax rates, etc.

You can print this tab out and give it to potential investors; it'll explain all the key assumptions in your model. You should resist ever giving a potential lender or investor a working version of the model. Even if the model is "bulletproof" (is completely free of errors), you're giving the potential investors an easy way to invent scenarios that will be overly pessimistic or that can otherwise be used against your best interests in some way.

Revenue

This tab will calculate your revenue for all product or service buckets, on a monthly basis, using figures contained on the *Assumptions* tab. If you prefer, it can also calculate associated figures, such as receivables balances and bad debt allowance.

The best way to calculate revenue is to set up assumptions on the productivity of your various sales channels (field salespeople, Internet sites, direct mail, and so on), and then calculate these on the *Revenue* tab. Seasonality can also be done here, but the seasonality assumptions should be on the *Assumptions* tab.

Gross Profit/Gross Margin

This tab will calculate the gross profit[29] or gross margin for each product or service bucket on a monthly basis, using the revenue from the *Revenue* tab and the gross profit/gross margin figures from the *Assumptions* tab.

Staffing

This tab will lay out the various positions that already exist within your company and those that may be added later. For clarity, organize them within departments, so a given position can be found more easily. You can set up conditions in the worksheet to not add a particular position unless certain conditions are fulfilled, such as:

- Date: Add this position at a certain date.
- Cash Flow or Cash Balance: Add this position when and if the company reaches a certain cash position.
- Revenue Level: Add this position when and if the company hits a defined revenue target.

Your *Assumptions* tab can contain these assumptions plus the salary levels, like the example shown above. You can also use this tab to total up the salary costs for each month and then add in the cost of payroll taxes and benefits to get total loaded cost. Don't forget to allow for regular pay increases for your staff.

Overhead (SG&A[30]) Expenses

This tab will take input from your *Staffing* tab and your *Assumptions* tab to put together all your operating costs. When doing this for the first time, set out a list of the bills you pay each month and use those for setting up categories (Rent, Utilities, Telephone Expense, etc.) and anticipated monthly amounts. If you're starting from scratch, you'll probably find it helpful to talk to an outside accountant who serves businesses like yours to get an idea of common types and amounts of expenses.[31] When in doubt, include a category and a reasonable expense estimate. While this will lower your profitability and cash flow, you'll gain credibility with the readers of your plan for being conservatively high with expense estimates.

Some operating expenses (telecommunications, office supplies) tend to increase as employees are added, while others (utilities, most types of insurance) will tend to stay flat or jump from one flat level to another, where they'll stay for a while.

Capital Expenditures (Fixed Asset Purchases)

Like everything else, drive this off your assumptions tab. In this case, the assumptions will relate to the amount of capital (fixed asset) expenditures in each period, which types of assets will be purchased, and their depreciable lives.

One way to do this is to determine what percent of revenue each year will have to be spent on various types of fixed assets (computer systems, manufacturing equipment, etc.). Through Internet research you may be able to determine what typical levels of "CAPEX" (capital expenditures) are as a percent of revenue for companies in your type of business. See Table 6.5 for an example.

You may need some help from an accountant in this area, particularly in the determination of depreciable lives. Depending on the type of asset, there will be a minimum and a maximum depreciable life; generally you'll want to choose as short a depreciable life as possible to front-load the deductions you can take in the earlier years. Your accountant's advice will be helpful in this area.

Principal and Interest

Based on the figures you set up in the *Assumptions* tab, this tab will calculate the interest and principal payments associated with different loans. For proper accounting treatment, this tab can also separate the amount you owe on the different loans into "current" (what you have to pay in the next twelve months) and "long-term" amounts. You'll need these numbers to put together your balance sheet in the forecast.

Table 6.5
Forecasting the Cost of Fixed Assets

	2008	2009	2010	2011	2012
Total CAPEX as % of Revenue	**8.50%**	**12.00%**	**14.00%**	**10.20%**	**9.25%**
CAPEX Components by Year:					
Manufacturing Equipment	45.00%	25.00%	20.00%	17.50%	17.50%
Automation Investments	10.00%	30.00%	40.00%	30.00%	25.00%
Back Office Systems	25.00%	30.00%	32.00%	40.00%	40.00%
Vehicles	10.00%	0.00%	5.00%	7.00%	10.00%
Other CAPEX	10.00%	15.00%	3.00%	5.50%	7.50%
	100.00%	100.00%	100.00%	100.00%	100.00%

A typical way to set this up in your *Assumptions* tab is to show the amount of debt, its term (the length of time until it will be paid off), its annual interest rate, and the date it will begin. This is all the information you need to calculate all the factors discussed in the paragraph above.

You might also have a revolving line of credit based on receivables or inventory. The terms for this can be put into the *Assumptions* tab, along with figures for the maximum limit available.

Financial Forecast

The prior tabs have all the information the model needs to produce forecasted financial results. These results include the three basic types of financial statements:

- Profit and Loss/Income Statement
- Balance Sheet
- Cash Flow/Source and Use of Funds

The P&L (Income) statement will be fairly straightforward to construct, as the revenue, direct costs, operating expenses, and so on can be taken off the preceding tabs. Constructing a correct and logical balance sheet and cash flow requires a thorough understanding of accounting principles. The logic behind this must be carefully constructed so that even radical changes in your assumptions (substituting equity investment for debt, accelerating investor buyouts, etc.) can be accommodated without sacrificing accuracy.

What you'll probably actually have are a number of tabs covering the financial forecast, but the key tab will be the monthly financial forecast of all three types of financial statements. All the calculations will be done on this tab. You can then use it as a source for producing quarterly and annual summaries as needed.

Now let's look at a general presentation layout for each of the three major types of financial statements your plan must produce.

PROFIT AND LOSS/INCOME STATEMENT

Table 6.6 shows what your profit and loss (or "income statement") might look like, in a skeleton framework. The lines would be labeled similarly. You'd typically have columns of figures for current month actual, current month budget/forecast, and the variance in both dollars and percent. You might also have a set of similar columns for year-to-date data.

You'll notice in the above example that at several key points there's a line inserted to measure some of the key figures (gross profit/gross margin, operating costs, operating income and net income) as a percent of revenue. This will serve as a handy guide to how your profitability is performing in certain key areas.

Table 6.6
A Framework for Showing Profit and Loss

Revenue (Sales)
  Less Bad Debt
Net Revenue
Less Direct Costs:
  Cost of Goods Purchased
  Sales Commissions
  Other Direct Costs
    Total Direct Costs
Gross Profit/Gross Margin
    As % of Net Revenue
Operating Costs
  Salaries
  Rent and Leases
  Travel and Entertainment
  Sales and Marketing
  Communications
    Total Operating Costs
    As % of Net Revenue
Operating Income (EBITDA)
    As % of Net Revenue
  Depreciation and Amortization
  Interest Expense
  Interest Income
Pre-Tax Income
  Federal Income Taxes
  State Income Taxes
Net Income
    As % of Net Revenue

BALANCE SHEET

Table 6.7 is an example of the structure of your balance sheet in your forecast. Each of the major blocks will have a number of subcategories that will be shown. For example, "Current Assets" will include cash, accounts receivable, inventory, and prepaid expenses. Typically you don't show budget comparisons and variances with balance sheet figures.

Table 6.7
Block Structure to Forecast Balance Sheet

Current Assets	Current Liabilities
Fixed Assets	Long-Term Liabilities
Other Assets	Equity

CASH FLOW/SOURCE AND USE OF FUNDS STATEMENT

This will be a key statement for your lenders and potential investors. Neither the profit and loss nor the balance sheet gives a good picture of how cash is actually flowing in and out of your business. There are several reasons for this, including:

- The timing differences between when you earn revenue or incur expenses and when cash actually changes hands.
- Principal payments on loans (principal payments aren't included as an expense in the income statement).
- Cash infusions from loans or investments.
- Purchase of major assets for your company (buildings, machinery, land, computer systems). These aren't shown as an expense on the income statement, but are "capitalized" and depreciated over an estimated lifetime).

A cash flow (or "Source and Use of Funds") statement will look something like Table 6.8.

You can see that some of these items, such as the Net Income figure at the top and the depreciation and amortization, come directly from your income statement. Others, such as the starting cash balance, changes in bank loans, etc., come from balance sheet information. The cash flow statement pulls them all together, and takes into account the effects on cash flow

Table 6.8
Typical Source and Use of Funds Statement

Net Income
   Adjustments to Net Income
   Depreciation and Amortization
   Decreases in Accounts Receivable
   Decreases in Other Current Assets
   Increases in Accounts Payable and Payroll
Net Cash Provided from Operations
   Investing Activities
   Ongoing Capital Investments
   Other Acquistion Activities
Cash Used in Investing Activities
Financing Activities
   Net Change in Bank Loan
   Transaction Costs
   Payoff of Participating Preferred
   Venture Capital Injections
Cash Provided by Financing Activities
Net Cash Flow
Cash Balance @ BOP
Cash Balance @ EOP

caused by capital investments, working capital cash flows, and so on. The "Net Cash Flow" near the bottom of that statement is one of the key figures your lenders and investors will focus on.[32]

FINANCIAL RATIOS

Whether you're approaching a bank, a venture capital firm, or potential individual investors, they'll want to calculate some standard financial ratios to see how your company's financial results stack up with comparable companies in the same industry.

The first step in this is to find out, if you don't already know, what the appropriate NAICS[33] (North American Industry Classification System) number for your company is. This will be a number up to six digits. See Appendix D for the link to this site and how to use it.

You can then use this number to access comparative studies for companies in the same line of business. Some of these may be available in a large public library, others through a university library, and a few on a paid subscription basis. You probably don't want to pay for a subscription for a one-time use, so if you can't find them in a public library, try going to a university library to locate them or, if you want to spend a little money to save time, hire a graduate or upper-division finance student to do your research for you using the university library's resources.

You'll build a great deal of credibility if you include the calculated financial ratios in your financial model along with comparatives for other companies in the same line of business (NAICS code). This may not really save them time (they'll go ahead and check your calculations), but it will improve their opinion of your financial sophistication. See Appendix A (Financial Ratios) for a list and description of the common ratios potential lenders or investors will want to look at.

Creativity in Your Ratios

Besides calculating the standard financial ratios laid out in Appendix A, you should also consider putting in some creative ratios that apply more specifically to your business and your industry. These are sometimes called "key levers." If you can identify those through research (see below) and incorporate them into your plan, comparing your company to its competitors, your credibility will take a huge leap upwards.

If you aren't sure what these might be, you might start by reading some of the publications related to your specific industry. This might also give you some insight into the ratios of some of your competitors, which you can include in your business plan to show that you've done some competitive analysis.

Some examples of ratios that might be applicable could include:

- Revenue per employee
- Or (perhaps a better ratio)—Revenue per payroll dollar

- Average revenue per customer, divided by revenue bucket
- Gross per margin per customer, divided by revenue bucket
- Web revenue per hit (visit)
- Customer retention statistics (for companies with subscribers)

Custom ratios like these will demonstrate your grasp of the unique essentials of your business and of the economics of your industry.

GRAPHS

It seems that lenders and investors now expect to see graphs as part of your presentation. It's easy to go overboard in this area, inundating the reader with dozens of graphs showing every set of numbers and trends in the model.

Keep your graphs to no more than half a dozen, and choose those carefully. One of the main advantages of graphs is to easily show key trends in your forecast. Therefore, most (if not all) of your graphs will be "time series" charts that show how a particular measure behaves over each year of your forecast.

A reasonable set of graphs might show trends in:

- Revenue (separated by bucket, if appropriate).
- Gross margin and operating income/EBITDA (combined on one chart).
- Cash flow and cash balances (combined on one chart).
- Some trends in important standard financial ratios.
- Some trends in customized ratios or "key lever" measures particular to your business.

THE "FINISHED VERSION" OF THE MODEL

Let's say that now, based on the guidelines set out here and on a lot of hard work by you and your staff, you now have what you've been assured is the final version of the model. Check for these items to make sure the model will reliably project your financials according to the rules you've set up:

- All these tabs should be organized the same way, with monthly columns and rows setting out each of the figures you're inputting or calculating. This will make it easy to keep the formulas that refer to these cells consistent.
- Once all the supporting tabs are set up, the actual financial part of the model can be built fairly simply. Instead of having complex formulas, it can just draw most of its data from the different supporting tabs.
- Make sure the person or company you use to put the entire model together can produce a complete set of financial projections. These must include monthly forecasts of your profit and loss (income statement), cash flow, and balance sheet. Have them show you examples of similar

projects they've done for other clients. The professionals you're talking to should be worried about client confidentiality here,[34] but it should be simple for them to eliminate client names and change key assumptions so that you're seeing an example without any confidential information.

- You should go through multiple iterations of the model to make sure the assumptions are realistic and give believable results. Building the model as outlined above, based on an *Assumptions* tab, will make these changes easy.
- Have an outside party with some financial background look over the results your model is showing to see if they seem realistic. The picture you want your financial forecast to convey to your potential lender or investor is that of a business which:
  - Understands the economics that drive the revenue and costs.
  - Takes a reasonable view of how it will grow the revenue of the business.
  - Uses conservative (not overly optimistic) assumptions.
  - Compares reasonably with other companies in the same line of business.

Once you've come up with a final "most likely" business plan, it'd be prudent to prepare two other views of the business. Potential investors, particularly those considering equity contributions, will want to understand what your financial results might look like under other conditions. They'll probably especially want to see a more pessimistic view of the company's results. You can do this easily by creating a different version of the plan using changes in your key assumptions. (Microsoft Excel has a feature called Scenario Manager that makes this relatively easy.)

Finally, once the model appears complete and has the scenarios built in, you'll want to test drive the model. You should start playing with the assumptions and make sure the model behaves correctly and predictably for even major changes in assumptions. Look for these factors during your test drive, which should be a lengthy exercise:

- Does the balance sheet always balance? In a well-built and complete model, no change you make should cause the total assets to NOT equal the total liabilities and equity. If this happens, there's a fundamental flaw with the model that must be fixed.
- See what happens to cash flow if you radically increase your revenue growth (you can use the "multiplier" in the revenue assumptions section to do this easily). You might be surprised to see it decrease, rather than increase. This could be a reasonable result because of increased capital spending, too much cash tied up in receivables, or too rapid payment of payables, decreasing your cash balances. Look at these results skeptically and insist that your expert prove to you that these results make sense.
- When you make a favorable change that should increase profitability, does the profit move in the correct direction? Does the amount that it moved seem reasonable based on the degree of change you made?

- The same consideration should hold for making unfavorable changes.
- Check the cash flow and how it behaves when you change assumptions regarding days of receivables and days of payables. When you increase days of receivables, cash flow should decrease, with the opposite being true for days of payables.
- Instead of making a number of changes simultaneously, make one at a time and see if the model's behavior seems logical and consistent. If you make several changes at the same time and then re-run it, you'll have a much more difficult time telling if the result is logical, or what specific change appeared to cause the problem.

CONCLUSION: YOU CAN MAKE IT HAPPEN

The main goal of this chapter is to help you understand what sorts of financial information will be expected by lenders or investors, and how you can produce that information. For business owners or key managers who haven't had exposure to the financial aspects of running a business, some of the terms and concepts may seem daunting. Most of them are really common sense, sometimes dressed up with terms that make them sound more complicated than they really are.

You'll need to pay particular attention to the concepts covered in this chapter before you approach a potential investor or lender. If you feel you have enough background and understanding to start digging into the process of putting together your financial plan, you'll be ready to present your business plan and raise some money to get your dream underway.

While there are a number of good books on this subject, you may find that the best way to get a better understanding is to take classes at a local college or university. You can usually pay an "auditing" fee to just sit in on the class and participate, but without getting a grade for it. This may be a good way to learn more about finance. Who knows? You might end up enjoying it as much as we do.

NOTES

1. Some of the reasons for this include non-cash expenses such as depreciation, cash expenditures that aren't treated as expenses, such as investments in equipment, and the "float" time between the time a bill is rendered and when it's paid.

2. An S corporation is really just a tax variant of the C corporation. Permission from the IRS is needed for this type of company.

3. There are kits readily available in bookstores that make it easy for a relatively inexperienced person to set up an LLC in her or his state. However, if you're planning on adding equity investors, you should work with an experienced attorney in forming your LLC.

4. "Secured" just means that the loan is guaranteed to a certain extent by granting a lien based on collateral, usually property such as a home, business

assets (accounts receivable, inventory, equipment), or an investment or savings account. "Unsecured" refers to a loan granted without collateral.

5. SBA = Small Business Administration. This is a special section of the federal Commerce Department which focuses on issues related to—what else?—small businesses. This includes loan guarantees, which can make it easier to gain debt financing. Talk to your banker or your closest SBA office about this. Also, check out the SBA's website (see Appendix D for the URL).

6. "Bank," in this context, could also mean other lending institutions, including specialized asset-based lenders.

7. An SBA guarantee, mentioned earlier, may be a good solution for business owners who are short of collateral. Please understand that this "guarantee" doesn't remove any personal liability from the business owner(s)—it actually adds another layer of liability, because if you default on the loan, you're likely to find the Federal government, in the name of the SBA, after you to make good the default.

8. A "good depositor" is a client who keeps his account well-funded, not incurring penalties or fees from the bank for overdrafts or other financial mistakes. As part of a good depository relationship, the bank would also like to have your business rely on them for company credit cards, retirement accounts, and so on.

9. VC firms may demand a potential return of up to 10 times their investment within a few years. This would translate to a phenomenally high annual rate of "interest."

10. Strictly speaking, "risk" and "uncertainty" are two different concepts. "Risk" represents a situation where the probabilities can be measured, such as in coin-flipping or most gambling situations. "Uncertainty" exists where there are several possible outcomes, but the probability of each one isn't known.

11. This collateralization would allow a lender to seize the asset that's been used as collateral. This extra degree of protection results in lower risk and therefore a lower interest rate than a non-collateralized loan.

12. It also imposes a lot of legal and financial obligations on the issuing company. Because of these obligations, many successful companies remain privately held.

13. "Book value per share," stated simply, is merely the total equity value in the company at a particular point in time divided by the number of shares of stock (or "units," in the case of an LLC) at the same point in time.

14. A "fixed" cost refers to costs that don't vary substantially over time or with revenue levels. Other than contractual obligations such as a bank loan or a real estate lease, few expense categories are really fixed.

15. I have to brag that I actually once had great success for a fairly long period using a statistical method (linear regression). I was projecting monthly revenue for our company in five different European countries with extremely high seasonal swings. My forecast, after seven months, was within 1 percent of actual results in all five countries. This was what we financial professionals refer to as "luck," because any change in market conditions would render my method useless, as they did in month 8.

16. For a retail business that's open on weekends and holidays, this obviously doesn't apply. However, you might want to take account of events such as long weekends when your customers may travel out of town.

17. It's true that you might have good reason to believe that future bad debt will be at a lower percent of revenue than current bad debt is, but so long as you're selling on credit terms, there WILL be some amount of bad debt risk inevitably associated with revenue.

18. From an accounting standpoint, your monthly allowance for bad debt (an expense or "contra-revenue" item) is added to a balance sheet item called "Reserve for Bad Debt." When an account has to be written off, the write-off amount is deducted from this reserve. If you've overestimated, you'll be able to recover the overestimated portion and recognize it as revenue.

19. This should be done every month, not just when you're doing the business plan. This regular exercise will help keep your bad debt accrual and your reserve in line with reality.

20. Gross margin (or gross profit—they're the same thing) equals revenue minus direct costs. Besides being expressed in absolute dollar terms, they're also often calculated as a percent of revenue. This should be done for each revenue bucket, so you can easily see the profit margins for each bucket.

21. In fact, an economic definition of "long run" is "in terms of operating activities, a period of time in which all costs are variable" (see http://www.answers.com/topic/long-run).

22. Commissions will vary with revenue, so your commission calculation in this sheet should be linked to your forecasted revenue level.

23. Some payroll taxes, such as federal unemployment and FICA (Social Security) have annual salary ceilings after which the company share disappears. Depending on the compensation level of your employees and how exactly you want to model payroll taxes, you may want to add this feature into your staffing model.

24. "Operating income" is your gross margin minus your operating costs. This is also known as "EBITDA" or "earnings before interest, taxes, depreciation and amortization."

25. By an "external" assumption, I mean a figure that's separate from the formula using it. As an example, let's say you wanted to grow a certain figure by 2.5 percent a month. One way to do it is to write a formula for each month that multiplies the prior month's figure by 1.025. If you wanted to change this to 3.5 percent, you'd have to change all the formulas. An external assumption would have a cell labeled "Monthly Expense Growth Rate" with the figure "2.5%" next to it. The formula for each month's expense would refer back to this cell. If you want to change the rate, you change only the reference cell. This also makes the model easier to understand and explain.

26. I strongly urge you to insert a "multiplier number" in the revenue section of the Assumptions tab. Set up the logic so that all the base assumptions are multiplied by this figure to get to the actual figures used in calculating revenue. The default setting will be 100%, but you can insert figures such as 75%, 150%, etc., to see the effect on your results.

27. This is another good place to have a multiplier like the one suggested above for revenue. In this case, the multiplier for direct cost is pessimistic if it goes **up**, since this means your ratio of cost to revenue increases.

28. For example, you can use simple assumptions such as "days of receivables" to calculate the accounts receivable balance for each month. These can be

separated by revenue category and can have trends built into their assumptions.

29. "Gross Profit" (generally used in manufacturing and retail operations) or "Gross Margin" are both defined as gross revenue minus all direct/variable costs. This is the amount you've netted on a given product or service (or on total operations) before your overhead/operating costs.

30. "SG&A" means "Sales, General and Administrative" expenses, or your overhead costs. Think of it as all the bills you have to pay other than the direct cost of your products and services.

31. These divisions should be reflected in your company's "Chart of Accounts." Take a look at it and make sure that the operating expense categories reflect the way you want things divided up.

32. The "BOP" and "EOP" on the "Cash Balance" rows at the bottom refer to "Beginning of Period" and "End of Period."

33. The NAICS system was devised in the late 1990s to replace the old SIC (Standard Industrial Classification) system. The hyperlink cited in Appendix D will also show the equivalent old SIC numbers. Make a note of your "old" SIC number—this will be handy if you use the SEC's "EDGAR" database to look for public financial reports on other companies in your industry.

34. If they freely give you samples of other clients' plans that haven't been "sanitized" by removing the names and altering the figures, you should strongly consider **not** using them. They might do the same with your plan. You need to make sure that your outside advisers have a strong sense of ethics, particularly in not sharing confidential information about your company with other people without your permission.

7

Writing in the Twenty-First Century: A Guide to Today's New Mechanics

Just hold them for a few innings, fellas. I'll think of something.
Charlie Dressen, former Brooklyn Dodgers manager

Few people disagree that the end of the twentieth century and the beginning of the new century brought unprecedented change to the world's countries and cultures. We saw the rise of computers and cell phones. The Internet is now as commonplace as electric power. E-mail and Instant Messaging have replaced memos and reports across the globe.

And like the clanking cans on strings behind a "Just Married" couple's car, grammar rules and punctuation have been dragged along for the ride, battered but still making noise.

Meanwhile, conversational English has become the de facto language for international business across all cultures. These new speakers of English, coupled with enormous technical innovations, have turned the language into a dynamic new communications tool that disdains the old ways. If U have ever typed a quick txt msg, or were too wired to sleep, or kicked an idea up a notch while thinking out of the box, or installed a dish so you can catch all the games on ESPN 24/7, then you can turn around and welcome the rest of us to this brave new world. (Your grandparents would not have understood any of the previous sentence—that's how much English has changed in the last few decades.)

On the heels of these changes we all suddenly realize how interconnected we now are—and what connects us is the rapidly adapting English language.

I approach modern English grammar and punctuation as a classicist. I revere Shakespeare for making up two or three new words with every play he wrote. I acknowledge the value of precise English, brought to a fine point by grammarians such as John Donne and Dr. Samuel Johnson. But even these worthies would tremble at the impact that blended languages and satellite communications have brought upon us. The English of Wordsworth and Milton, of Jefferson and Franklin, is no longer spoken. One needs a teacher nowadays to explain the word usage of Walt Whitman.

We are in a new age of functional grammar rules—we go with whatever works. This is fair. The language culture has changed, and the rules of grammar serve language. After all, the entire point of "correct" writing is that you are not along to explain to the reader what you mean. Your word choice, usage, and punctuation must explain your meaning for you. When you converse with someone, you do not say "comma" or "dash" or anything of the sort to convey meaning. You let vocal inflection and pauses do that work for you. Since we live in an age of relaxed, informal speech, our new grammar rules simply reflect this new reality.

For those of us who write business plans and proposals, the new reality is a challenge. We often do not know our readers. Do they know English as a second language? Are they likely to be offended by our inconsistent use (say) of a semicolon, or will it not bother them at all? Will our use of good English enhance our prospects of getting approval or financing or the contract? All good questions worth pursuing.

I have put this chapter purposely between plans and proposals because it applies equally to both. If you follow the guidelines here, your chances of writing clear, action-generating prose will be greatly enhanced. So let's take a look at what's still in use and what's new in grammar and punctuation. We'll start with the macro view and get—as the techies say—granular.

STYLE GUIDES ANSWER MOST QUESTIONS

A good contemporary style guide is the writer's best friend. They range from formal (*Modern Language Association*) to semi-formal (*Chicago Manual of Style*) to downright folksy (*The Complete Idiot's Guide to Grammar and Style*). Journalists (who used to be called "reporters") tend to use the *Associated Press Stylebook*. Two other guides that are unpretentious and current are *Working with Words: A Handbook for Media Writers and Editors*, and the *Broadview Pocket Guide to Writing*.

Every organization from IBM to Dixie's Doggie Daycare needs a style guide, whether you buy one off the shelf or write it yourself. I have advised some firms to write their own because their industry has arcane or specialized usage of words and expressions. For most of us, however, off the shelf is fine.

So browse. Find one you like, and make it your official guide. Then insist that people in the organization use and follow the guide. A style guide makes all of the petty and annoying decisions about usage for you, so that every document coming out of your organization looks as if it came from a single source. This builds synergy for your organization and is critical in our new age.

For example, take that good gray lady, the *New York Times*. Every story, every op-ed piece, every essay is written in the same grammar and punctuation style for consistency. Every man is called Mr. Smith or Dr. Smith; every woman is called Ms. Jones or Dr. Jones. The hundreds of writers who work for the *Times* don't have to waste time pondering whether to use or not use "Mr." in front of a man's name. The paper has decided in advance for you. Do you use "twenty" or "20" in the middle of a sentence? The paper has decided for you. Do you use "FBI" or "F.B.I."? And so on. A style guide has a positive and powerful cumulative effect on readers, and you need one.

Let's say you provide contract work for the U.S. Navy. Do you write "Commander in Chief, Pacific Fleet" every time, or "CINCPACFLT"? Do you write "Admiral" or "Adm."? Do you write "USS" or "U.S.S."? Having your own custom style guide here is essential.

If you deal with hospital personnel, do you write "Doctor" or "Dr."? Is it "Nurse Williams," "Emily Williams, R.N.," "E. Williams, RN," or some other construction? It doesn't really matter which it is, but it matters that you are consistent.

Are abbreviations allowed? Should we write "25 June 20XX" or "June 25, 20XX" or "6/25/20XX"? Is it "third" or "3rd"? These are small considerations in this moment, but over many years of organizational communications they take on significance.

Of greater import for you and your organization is that a pleasing consistency in style makes your documents easily searchable by others. A prospect, in other words, will be pleased to see such useful consistency. Again, one of the books mentioned above will give you a good start—you don't need to reinvent the wheel on the basic items like how to present numbers or titles. The authors of such books have seen it all—and made rules to cover nearly every contingency.

HANDBOOKS HELP WITH PUNCTUATION AND GRAMMAR

All professional writers have an English usage handbook or two on their shelves. I have seven, and I use them frequently. A good handbook provides answers to the essential questions regarding usage, grammar, and punctuation. Do you put in a comma before the last "and" in a series, or leave it out? A handbook will advise you. (I recommend that you always put it in.) Do you hyphenate two adjectives used as a single modifier to a noun? Check the handbook. When do you hyphenate words that end in "ly"? Handbook, again.

All professions have handbooks or manuals that guide practitioners in the proper use of their tools. Doctors have the *Physicians' Desk Reference*. Lawyers have *Gladstone*. Mechanics have manuals for every make and model of automobile and truck. Writers have handbooks. The best ones are regularly updated by the publishers every two or three years. I have used *The Business Writer's Handbook,* by Brusaw, et al., for my entire career. *The Gregg Reference Manual* is a solid handbook with clear examples and a well-organized index. Check out one or two at a bookstore and add them to your library. Then please use them.

This being the twenty-first century, writers have excellent online resources as well. They are too numerous to mention even all the best of them. One of the most popular grammar and punctuation websites is wsu.edu/

~brians/errors/index.html. It is maintained gleefully and magnanimously by Prof. Paul Brians at Washington State University. One of my favorites for building vocabulary is ProofReadNow.com. This company provides professional proofreading services for a fee. However, if free is what you're looking for, its monthly newsletter on vocabulary is both invigorating and inspiring. And for a longer list of sites, try WritersDigest.com/101sites/. After all that, if you just want to have fun at a literary site, try www.bartleby. com. Named after Melville's melancholy scrivener, this is a useful guide to literature.

DICTIONARIES ARE A CONTEMPORARY GUIDE TO WORD USAGE

Dictionaries: You should have one.

For business professionals, a recent paperback will do. I prefer collegiate editions as they tend to be current on how the younger generation is talking. *The American Heritage Dictionary of the English Language* has excellent usage notes and includes a CD-ROM to ease the burden of business travelers.

Further, many universities will allow visitors to link to their libraries and a variety of dictionaries. And don't forget Dictionary.com if you're in a hurry.

In addition: a thesaurus, a spelling guide, a few books on grammar and effective phraseology and letter writing, and a revised *Elements of Style* by Strunk & White should round out your library nicely.

CLARITY, MEET CONSISTENCY—CONSISTENCY, MEET COMMON SENSE

Contemporary writing style is all about being clear quickly. Modern readers will forgive minor grammatical lapses, as long as we get on with it. Here's a construction I see every day: "Everyone must turn in their time-sheets before the end of each week."

Miss Bingham, my 11th-grade English teacher of blessed memory, would have sent me to study hall for writing such a sentence. Singular antecedents take singular pronouns, of course. And so everyone must turn in his or her timesheets, since "everyone" is singular. Miss Bingham, alas, is no longer with us, and neither is her abhorrence of such a construction. In fact, "their" is fast taking the place of the awkward "his or her" in business usage. It was bound to happen: We need a pronoun for a non-gender-specific singular antecedent, and "they" or "their" works nicely for English. Other languages, such as German, have similarly useful constructs. I have seen such pronouns used routinely in formal business plans and proposals; it is still considered casual English, but it works.

The rules are easing up. Here are some rules that have loosened or gone away in the last several decades.

- Ending Sentences with Prepositions. Readers don't worry so much about this one anymore, so long as you don't overdo it. For example: "Hector thought about the man he would compete against." This ends in a preposition, and is perfectly fine. To avoid ending in a preposition, we might write: "Hector thought about the man against whom he would compete." Again, perfectly fine, if slightly stuffy. Her Majesty the Queen might prefer it, but you are not likely to be writing to her anytime soon.
- Splitting Infinitives. The infinitive is the "eternal" form of a verb (the one you find when you look it up) combined with "to," as in: to run, to act, to confer. Miss Bingham and her ilk were stern about not allowing a random adverb to come between the "to" and the verb, as in "to boldly go," perhaps the most famous split infinitive in all of Star Fleet. The unsplit form, "to go boldly," sounds slightly non-military and not at all like Captain Kirk. Here's another example: "She agreed immediately to book the conference room for next week." The infinitive is not split, and it sounds right. So when will she book the room? We don't know. Perhaps next year. It is only her agreement that is immediate. One good way to know exactly when she will reserve the room is to split the infinitive: "She agreed to immediately book the conference room for next week." Splitting the infinitive is perfectly legal, so split away.
- Using Contractions. Contractions—like it's for it is, once considered too informal for business use—are now commonplace in all but the highest level of legal contracts. Use them discreetly in proposals and plans and no one'll complain. (Well, almost everyone will complain about that last one.)

Splitting infinitives and ending sentences in prepositions have never really been mistakes. But some people (your boss among them, no doubt) still think they are mistakes. So tiptoe carefully through these tulips, and discuss these issues with your team ahead of time.

Some rules of grammar and punctuation, however, are still in place, if less draconian than earlier decades, and so let's deal with them now.

BASIC GRAMMAR

What follows is a quick review of how grammar works. This will be painless. It will not be exhaustive, however. For that, you need a handbook.

Subjects and Predicates

To be complete, a sentence needs two elements: a subject and a predicate. The subject is the topic, or what the sentence is about. The predicate tells something about the subject.

(1) *Jeremy* distributed the quarterly report.

In sentence (1), "Jeremy" is the subject and "distributed the quarterly report" is the predicate. The sentence is about "Jeremy" and what he did with the report. If we were to diagram the sentence, to reduce it to its essence, it would be: "Jeremy distributed report." The words "the" and "quarterly" are adjectives describing the report.

From here the sentence can get as complex as the writer wants.

(2) *Jeremy and his marketing-department cohorts* distributed the quarterly report.

(3) *Jeremy, along with Peyton and Cameron, his marketing-department cohorts,* distributed the quarterly report to a bewildered and unsettled board of directors. (The essential sentence is still "Jeremy distributed report.")

(4) *An abashed Jeremy, along with Peyton and Cameron, his marketing-department cohorts,* distributed the quarterly report on heavy, cream-colored stock to a bewildered and unsettled board of directors whose temper the beautifully printed pages failed to ameliorate.

The essential sentence is still—you guessed it—"Jeremy distributed report."

In each of these examples, the subject consists of everything except the predicate, "distributed etc."

The predicate consists of the verb, any complements or objects, and everything that modifies them. In this case, the verb is "distributed."

We express English in the major parts of speech. We have to understand how these categories are different in order to express ourselves correctly so that the reader or listener understands our meaning.

Parts of Speech

Noun: Name of a

- Person (Tyrone)
- Place (Greenville)
- Thing (ornament)
- Activity (golfing)
- Concept (gratitude)

"Yellowstone is a magnificent national *park."*
Noun compound: One noun modifies another

- Staff problems
- Press briefing
- Emergency management
- Airline food
- Building maintenance

Pronoun: Replaces a noun or noun phrase. Personal pronouns replace known nouns: I, me, my, mine, myself, you, your, yours, yourself, yourselves.

- It, its, itself
- She, her, hers, herself
- He, him, his, himself

- We, us, our, ours, ourselves
- They, them, their, theirs, themselves

Indefinite pronouns substitute for unknown or unspecified persons or things:

- Some, any, several, anybody, anything, nothing, nobody, one, no one, few, etc. (Note that some of these words can serve as adjectives when followed by a noun: any books, few people, several considerations, some pundits.)

Interrogative and relative pronouns:

- Who, whose, whom, whoever

Interrogative pronouns ask questions: Whose pen is this? Relative pronouns reference previously identified nouns: the person whose pen was left in the classroom has not yet been found.

If the noun comes before the pronoun, it is called its *antecedent*. If the antecedent is singular, the pronoun must be singular. If plural, the pronoun must be plural.

- Shirley and Jake have invited us to *their* apartment.
- Every resident of London likes *his or her* tea hot.

If the antecedent is used as a subject, the pronoun must be a subject pronoun. If the antecedent is used as an object, the pronoun must be an object pronoun.

For example, prepositional phrases always take the object pronoun. As in: "Between you and *me*, the rumor is true." "Me" is the object case. "I" is the subject case, and thus inappropriate in the example. However, we often hear people say "Between you and I ...". This is a wrong pronoun choice.

Verb: Expresses action, existence or occurrence. Verbs take a variety of forms, depending on the person and number of the subject and the time (tense) and aspect of the event or occurrence.

Adjective:

- Describes or limits a noun.
- Can serve as a noun (the British).
- Can take three forms: absolute, comparative, superlative (green, greener, greenest).

Adverb:

- Modifies anything but a noun or pronoun. (He photographed *carefully* a scene from Yellowstone, the magnificent national park.)
- Can also modify a whole sentence: "Frankly, Scarlett, I hate that dress!"

Preposition: has an adverbial or adjectival function.

- "Pre"-position: comes *before* a noun phrase.
- Preposition + noun phrase = prepositional phrase: "The brook runs *under* the bridge." "The calf walked *behind* its mother *at* the rear of the herd."

Conjunction:

- Coordinating (and, but, or).
- Subordinating (although, after, before, because, as, if, since, that, when, where, while, until, etc.).
- Correlative (either + or, neither + nor, both + and, not only + but also, whether + or).

She *and* I went to the cafeteria for lunch.

Jack read his report to us, *but* no one understood his conclusion.

Interjection: Worthy of mention but not worthy of use in semi-formal prose. They include words such as *Aha! Ouch!* and *Huh*! to express surprise or some other emotion. Please don't use interjections in business writing unless you are quoting someone else or going for a creative risk.

Participle: A verb phrase that functions as an adjective. "*Speaking carefully,* the boss gave us his view of last year's performance."

Gerund: A verb form that functions as a noun. It always ends in –*ing.* "The boss, *spinning,* shone the best possible light on our sales figures for the year."

REACHING AGREEMENT

The one area where most business writers make mistakes, in my experience, is in agreement. Subject and verb must agree. That is, if the subject is singular, the verb must be singular. "*Paula works* in accounting." Both Paula and works are singular. You would never say "Paula work in accounting." Similarly, pronoun and antecedent must agree. A plural noun takes a plural pronoun. "*Members* who participate in the conference will find something *they* like." If you understand agreement you can avoid most grammatical mistakes. The following examples contain errors of agreement. Please correct them. I provide the answers immediately after the examples. (Please notice that your software's spell-check function will miss many of these errors.)

Subject and Verb Agreement

1. A range of choices were made available to the technicians regarding shift assignments.
2. Ethics are the study of moral philosophy.
3. Neither of the creative department's ideas were acceptable.
4. Each of the assembly workers go outside for coffee and lunch breaks.

5. Twelve weeks are the normal length of our sales training efforts.
6. A series of sessions on customer-focused selling techniques were held in the offices of clients.

How Sentences Work

It is useful here to consider how sentences work. A sentence is the building block of prose. We express our thoughts in sentences.

In English, a sentence wants to go from left to right, subject to verb to object. This is the best construction for simplicity and understanding.

"Madison sent copies of the workbook to all participants."

The essential sentence is: Madison … sent … copies. "Of the workbook" and "to all participants" are prepositional phrases that add to the meaning, but are not essential.

In creating the structure of any sentence, determine the true subject, true verb, and true object (if there is one). Consider this little gem: "The use of our new Opal finance-management software program and manuals, while taking days to install, still offer far-ranging benefits." Can you spot the error? The verb needs to be singular, because the subject is singular. And what is the subject? It's what the sentence is about. The essence of the sentence is:

Use … offers … benefits.

Subject … verb … predicate.

"Use" is what the sentence is about and is singular; therefore, the verb needs to be singular: *offers*. One could write: "The many uses of our new Opal … offer … benefits." In that case a plural subject requires a plural verb.

What about the other parts of this sentence?

- "… of our new Opal finance-management software program and manuals" is a vast prepositional phrase that is not the subject.
- "… while taking days to install" is another appositive phrase, or a phrase that adds to the meaning but is not essential.
- And "far-ranging" is an adjective construction that modifies "benefits."

The challenge here is that there are sixteen words between the subject and verb. You will tend to make mistakes like subject/verb agreement unless you can understand the structure of the sentence in your head or on paper. The questions always are:

- What is the essential sentence?
- What is the subject?
- What is the verb?
- What (if any) is the object?

Pronoun and Antecedent Agreement

1. Either Jack or Paul will buy their ticket at the box office.
2. Each of the engineers has their own way of writing code.
3. A group of the newer sales representatives are wasting their time reviewing out-of-date brochures.
4. I'm sure everyone who participates in the conference will find something they like.

Subject and Verb Agreement–Answers

1. A range of choices WAS made available to the technicians regarding shift assignments. (*Range*, the subject, is singular.)
2. Ethics IS the study of moral philosophy. (*Ethics* is a single thing, not plural, even though it looks plural.)
3. Neither of the creative department's ideas WAS acceptable. (*Either/or* and *neither/nor* are coordinating conjunctions. In each case the noun phrase closest to the verb determines the form of the verb. "Either the CEO himself or his two top aides are attending the conference." OR: "Either the two top aides or the CEO himself is attending the conference.")
4. Each of the assembly workers GOES outside for coffee and lunch breaks. (*Each* is singular.)
5. Twelve weeks IS the normal length of our sales training efforts. (If *twelve weeks* is treated as a single grouping, the construct is singular. Compare these two: "Twenty-six miles *is* the length of a marathon." versus "Twenty-six miles *are* unpaved.")
6. A series of sessions on customer-focused selling techniques WAS held in the offices of clients. (*Series* is a single thing.)

Pronoun and Antecedent Agreement–Answers

1. Either Jack or Paul will buy HIS ticket at the box office.
2. Each of the engineers has HIS OR HER own way of writing code. (If the engineers are all male, "his" is fine.)
3. A group of the newer sales representatives IS wasting ITS time reviewing out-of-date brochures. (A group is a thing, an it.)
4. I'm sure everyone who participates in the conference will find something HE OR SHE LIKES.

BASIC PUNCTUATION

Punctuation rules, like grammar rules, are based on common sense. The business readers for whom you write look for basic punctuation skills and are content to let the higher transgressions alone. In addition, many business readers these days aren't so sure of punctuation themselves, making these good times to live in. Or if you prefer: good times in which to live.

That being said, most of the punctuation errors I see have to do with commas, semicolons, and hyphens. Most readers know the rules for using these; if you err, you are likely to lose a few points regarding your own seriousness of purpose. So let's take a look at these credibility killers, with a nod to colons, dashes, apostrophes, and quotation marks.

Using Commas

The lowly comma is the most misused and misunderstood of all punctuation marks. If you're going to make a mistake in your writing, chances are a comma will be involved. A comma separates, links, or clarifies. It sets apart and it introduces. Using it properly is vital for clear communications. Here are the main reasons for using a comma.

- To connect independent clauses. An independent clause is essentially a sentence, with a subject and verb. It can stand alone: "Proposal writing is among the highest of business skills, but so few people appreciate it." You use a comma to connect independent clauses *only if* the clauses are linked by a conjunction. (If there is no conjunction, use a semicolon, as I'll explain later.)
- To enclose elements. "The sales team's new manager, who began his duties last week, was himself a standout road warrior."
- To introduce clauses, phrases, adverbs, and so on. "Because this ice cream is sugar free, you can enjoy it without guilt." "Indeed, the tilde is an arcane mark." "The engineering team discovered, however, that the quality of the finish is still unacceptable." "In addition, we will include our exclusive coffee mug with your order." "Subsequently, the researchers made additional tests." (Note that you can often eliminate the comma by reordering: "The researchers subsequently made additional tests." Reordering is often the best way to walk around a punctuation problem that leaves you puzzled.)
- To separate items in a series. This is a hotly debated topic even today, as some experts advocate dropping the comma before the last *and* in a series. Most contemporary guides advise keeping the comma before the last *and*, because you can't go wrong this way. "Modern dieticians suggest we all go easy on sugar, flour, and tobacco for healthier lives."

Hard as it might be to believe, many cases have come to court because a comma was erroneously added or omitted. For example, say you are at the reading of the will of a friend who, sadly, passed away. Your name is Louise. The judge reads the following: "Please divide my fortune among Ted, Thelma, George and Louise." Do you get one-fourth of the treasure, or do you split a third of it with George? I say let's go to court.

Many do go to court. In 2006, a Canadian company had to pay an extra $2.3 million because of the misuse of a comma in one sentence of a contract. They thought the contract was for five years, but a misplaced comma let the other company off the hook in only one year. That's a hefty price to pay for the slip of a comma. And there's a moral to the story. If you don't believe in the absolute value of precise punctuation in a contract, the other side's lawyer does.

There are many other uses for commas. A good guide can explain them all to you. The most frequent comma error I see has to do with putting in a comma where the writer feels the need to take a breath. There is no rule that covers this. Here are some typical examples:

- "The engineer they plan to hire, is Joe Smith."
- "You can read the draft now or, when you arrive in the morning."

These are inappropriate uses of commas. You should avoid them. I advise my students to know the rule for using any punctuation mark, or else not to use it.

Using Semicolons

The semicolon is among the most sophisticated of punctuation marks. I recommend you use it freely. However, use it correctly or not at all. It is better to write simple, declarative sentences than to attempt something fancy and make a glaring error.

Play within your game.

I have learned a great deal about this important life principle from Fred C., a golf professional whose expertise I call on every so often. I went to him for instruction recently and he asked me what I wanted to work on.

"Fred, you know how Tiger Woods can hit a wedge shot eighty yards and make the ball dance backwards on the green?" I said.

"Yep," Fred said, a man of few words.

"Well," I said, "teach me how to do that."

Fred studied me for a moment, the way a biologist studies a new form of bacteria. "Dennis," he said, "out of fourteen fairways, how many can you hit off the tee in an average round?" There are eighteen holes in a round of golf, but typically four of them are par-threes. One's tee shot should hit the green on a par three, since all pars are based on two putts. (I use "should" in the same sense that I "should" be thirty pounds lighter.)

"Three," I said. The rest end up in the rough, in the lake, or on the wrong fairway.

"Hmmm," Fred said. "And out of eighteen greens, how many can you hit in regulation?"

"Same number," I said. "Three." The rest take more than the regulation number of shots to hit the bloody green. I am a duffer of the first rank—my career best is an eighty-four. Tiger Woods requires on average one stroke fewer per hole than I do, on his worst day.

"Okay," Fred said. "When you can hit eight fairways and ten greens in regulation, come see me and I'll teach you how to back up that ball for free."

Fred, in his kind and wise way, was telling me to play basic golf until I can shoot a round of seventy-seven, a feat not likely in the years I have left, given my feeble hand-eye coordination (except when I'm throwing putters into the lake—at that I'm dead on). I hope you can use Fred's wisdom in your writing. For clear communication, basic is all you need.

Now for the semicolon. There are only three reasons to use a semicolon.

1. To connect two independent clauses without the use of a conjunction:

    • "Martina will handle the financial reports; I'll write the introduction."
    • "The creative department is adding a copywriter and art director to the roster; our main client is growing and needs the additional strength from us."

2. To connect two independent clauses that use a transition word between them, such as however, moreover, and so on.

    • "Peyton led the team in sales this quarter; however, my profit-per-call rate is higher for the year."
    • "The team evaluated the above-described process; unfortunately, the finish was still unacceptable."

3. To separate items in a series when the series contains commas that might be confusing.

    • "I have booked a meeting with Joan Smith, CEO; Carl Perkins, CFO; Jim Wilson, COO; and Laurel Hudson, VP Sales."

Please note that the semicolon's finest work is to show relationships or close meaning. You use a semicolon to tell the reader that these clauses, although independent, are closely related. It is in the revealing of relationships that the semicolon truly shines. Use it in good health.

Using Hyphens

Consider this sentence: "Kim Balsam recently hired a fat processing engineer."

A hyphen's primary function is to cobble together two or three words and tell the reader they are to be used as one word. When the hyphen is not used properly we often get sad constructions as in the sentence above. Is it likely that Kim Balsam's new hire is overweight? In our fast-food culture that might indeed be the case, but not relevant to the engineer's skills. It is more likely that our new recruit is expert in the processing of fat. So to make the sentence clear we need to add a hyphen between *fat* and *processing*. Those two words are used as one adjective to modify the noun *engineer*.

"Kim Balsam recently hired a fat-processing engineer."

Without the hyphen the sentence is odd, even nonsensical. Without the hyphen we are saying that she hired a fat engineer who is a processing engineer, as each adjective stands alone.

Hyphens thus help to make your meaning crystal clear. Examples:

(1) "As a marketing specialist, I can help you maximize your new product advertising dollars." This sentence is confusing on its face. Without a hyphen, the reader cannot take the writer's meaning. We can guess, but cannot be sure which of two possible meanings the writer intended. Perhaps the writer meant this:

(2) "As a marketing specialist, I can help you maximize your new-product advertising dollars." In this case, the writer's expertise is in spending money effectively to advertise new products. Both *new* and *product* are used together, as one word, to modify dollars. Or perhaps the writer meant this:

(3) "As a marketing specialist, I can help you maximize your new product-advertising dollars." In this case, what's new is the money spent on advertising products. One presumes that before now the company has been spending its advertising money on services or perhaps on branding.

But those are two quite different meanings; the intended one is clear only with the proper use of a hyphen.

Hyphens have many other uses that a handbook can explain for you. For example, resent is not the same word as re-sent. Resign is different from re-sign. Hyphens often make prefixes and suffixes clear: anti-communist or governor-elect. In the vast majority of uses, hyphens link two or three words together—a boon for us working writers.

Here are some more wide-ranging examples of using hyphens to form complex adjectives. Thanks for these go to Steve Delchamps, a technical writer colleague who stresses that the point of grammar rules is to enhance common sense.

- noun + participle (heart-shaped)
- noun + gerund (a steam-cleaning process)
- adjective + participle (fine-grained, three-sided, above-mentioned)
- adjective + noun (high-velocity, low-cost)
- cardinal number + noun (two-part)
- number + dimension + adjective (a three-inch-wide margin)
- verb + preposition (We have a back-up plan.)
- self + gerund (self-correcting)
- quasi + adjective (quasi-rational)
- cardinal number + participle (five-pointed)

Using Colons

A colon alerts the reader that something important is pending. It introduces lists. It explains or describes. And it may be used to connect two independent clauses in a "firmer" way, so to speak, than a semicolon.

- Lists: "Jerry likes both kinds of music: country *and* western."
- Explains: "An advertising agency has two major functions: to help some clients make money and to help the rest of its clients make money."

- Connects firmly: "There is only one way to get his fingerprints: obtain a warrant."
- Headlines or titles are another major use for colons: "King Lear: A Tragedy in Five Acts"

Using Dashes

Writers use dashes the way chefs use hot peppers—for that little touch of "Woo!"

A dash substitutes for most of the other punctuation marks. It provides strong emphasis while doing so. The bad news is, just like hot peppers, you overuse the dash at your peril. If you have more than two dashes per printed page, you are using too many dashes.

Here is one of my favorite dash-using quotes from the master, Yogi Berra: "What made Mickey Mantle great was he could hit just as good right-handed as he could left-handed—he's naturally amphibious."

Dashes, like penguins, normally come in pairs. They mark an abrupt change in thought or a self-interruption, usually to emphasize a point: "Yesterday the committee—a hard-working group of non-experts—set forth four recommendations to improve next quarter's profits."

They are also well used to set off a list of items when the list contains commas: "She listed the qualities—intelligence, humor, self-deprecation— that she liked in a department head."

Using Apostrophes

An apostrophe is a little mark with a lot of power. We use it to show possession and to form contractions. It marks possession, but is never used to mark possession with personal pronouns.

Most of the mistakes I see have to do with the pronoun *it*. Take this sentence: "A bluebird chirps only to it's fellow bluebirds." Many readers would skim right over this without a bump. But the pronoun *it* is one of the rare cases when we use an apostrophe to show a contraction, not possession.

"A bluebird chirps only to its fellow bluebirds" is correct.

"It's a bluebird's chirp that we hear in the spring" is also correct—a contraction of *it is.*

Most of the time, however, an apostrophe shows possession, whether singular or plural. If singular, add an apostrophe and an s. When singular words or names end in an s, you may use an apostrophe without the s.

Singular:

- The provost's declaration
- The librarian's schedule
- Dennis' racket
- James Jones' report

When plural nouns end in *s*, add only the apostrophe. Plural nouns without an *s* ending take '*s*.
Plural:

- The supervisors' meeting
- The employees' cafeteria
- The children's area
- The men's volleyball team

Indefinite pronouns such as *everyone* and *someone* need '*s* to form the possessive; personal possessive pronouns do not.

- It was someone's mistake.
- It was nobody's responsibility.
- That laptop is theirs.
- The shoes are hers.

Complex organization names typically show possession on the last name.

- Smith & Wollensky's steaks are the finest.
- Amazon.com's books are easy to order.
- Horn and Hardart's sandwiches were fun to buy.
- Jackie and Betty's apartment is nearby (when they share an apartment).
- Jackie's and Betty's apartments are around the corner (when each has her own apartment).

In the good old days, say fifteen years ago, writers used to form the plural of numbers, letters and symbols with '*s*.

- Don't use %'s in formal reports.
- He scored two 7's on the last two holes.
- That was common practice back in the 1990's.

That usage seems to have gone away. Today we simply say "he scored two 7s on the last two holes" and "common practice back in the 1990s." Additionally, the AP stylebook advocates use of the '*s* construction when dealing with a single letter, as in the Oakland A's. Otherwise it would look like the Oakland As. I think this makes sense.

Using Quotation Marks

Quotation marks set off the exact words that someone has said or written:

- Juliet said that "a rose by any other name would smell as sweet."
- The boss gave me a report that "must be turned in by Friday."

In the United States, commas and periods typically go inside the closing quotation mark. Semicolons, colons, question marks and exclamation marks go outside if they are not part of the original quote.

- The boss says that "sales are slipping," but no one knows how to improve the picture.
- "What did the supervisor say?" he asked.
- Why did the supervisor say to "double the maintenance on Lathe #14"?

When you have a long quotation in your text (more than five lines, say), set it off by indenting and single-spacing it, without quotation marks. And use single quotation marks to set off a quote within a quote.

- The professor pointed out that "Shakespeare's use of 'rose by any other name' comes from ancient poetic tradition."

These are the most common usages in contemporary grammar and punctuation. You can see them reflected in the best magazines and journals being written today. For help when you need it, I strongly recommend that you find a good contemporary English handbook and keep it handy.

II

HOW TO WRITE A
BUSINESS PROPOSAL

8

Raise the Bar: What You Are Really Proposing

When you play this game 20 years, go to bat 10,000 times, and get
3,000 hits, do you know what that means? You've gone 0 for 7,000.
Pete Rose, baseball's all-time hit leader. Out of
14,053 at-bats, he had 4,256 hits.

A proposal is you, standing in front of a group of prospective clients or customers, making an impassioned plea for them to see things your way. You
are reading their body language for clues as to how the presentation is
going. You are careful to make it short enough to hold their attention. When
their eyelids start to droop, you click a colorful graphic onto the screen to
illustrate a point you're making. Or you punch up a rock track to help you
segue to the next point. You want to make sure you get all your selling
points across with a dash of personality and a few suggestions about the
unique advantages you and your company offer them.

Except—you're not standing in front of a group of people. You don't
have physicality or music or stunning visuals to grab their attention. You're
doing all of this in writing.

A PROPOSAL IS A PRESENTATION—IN PROSE

Now *that* is a true challenge. The world is full of business professionals
who can dazzle 'em with footwork and turn a live presentation into a
Hollywood production. That's easy. What's hard is to win the business
using only your writing skills.

So you have to "read" their body language while writing, using your
experience and imagination. You have to write short and strong sentences
to keep them reading. You have to time your subheads and graphics based
on your knowledge of how much time and attention business professionals
can give your efforts. And you want to convey your selling points within a
discussion of their needs. That's hard to do.

The essence of a Request for Proposal (RFP) or a Request for Quote
(RFQ) is that the prospect specifies that he or she does *not* want to see your

smiling face or the freshly scrubbed faces of your team. In fact, people who issue RFPs often insist that you not show up, that you not call, that you send your ideas to them on paper, before a certain deadline, if you want a shot at their business. If you make the first cut, odds are good that you'll get your chance to dazzle them in person. But for now it's just you and the printed page.

William Goldman, the screenwriter, in his wonderful book *Adventures in the Screen Trade*, writes about the challenges of evoking excitement in readers using only words. He illustrates one point with a passage from his famous *Butch Cassidy and the Sundance Kid.* It's the scene where Butch and Sundance, marooned in Bolivia and not happy about it, are fired upon by what seems like a brigade of soldiers. Goldman, in describing Sundance shooting and running, shooting and running, goes on for several pages—and it's all one sentence. He wants the reader to be as breathless as Sundance is, and that's what he gets. It's a masterful performance.

Of course I'm not suggesting you write a two-page sentence. But as a proposal writer, you face the same challenges a screenwriter faces while dropping a 200-page script over the transom, or a politician faces while writing a speech, or a novelist faces while trying to make you want to turn those pages. You're trying to generate some kind of action. You want your reader to *do* something.

Let's assume you are reading this book because you have to write a proposal soon. I'd like to suggest some ways for you to think about the task that might help motivate you to do a great job writing it. And then let's make a list of what—precisely—you might want the reader to do.

THE NUMBER-ONE SECRET OF PROPOSAL WRITING

Here it is. It's the best idea I can offer you in this entire book, and it is three little words:

Write about Them

"Well, sure, Dennis (I can almost hear you saying), of course it's about them. I know that. They are looking to me and my competitors to give them a solution to their problem that they can live with and succeed with. And I'll get to them, you bet I will. But first, they need to hear about the entire history of my company to give them, you know, some useful background."

Here's how I would respond to anyone who makes a comment like that: balderdash. Maybe even: horsefeathers. When a company issues an RFP, they care not one whit about you. They are consumed with themselves and their particular challenges. They need serious help with a serious problem. That's why they are issuing the RFP in the first place. They don't want to know about you, at least not initially. They want to know how you can help *them!*

If you don't believe me, maybe you'll believe Dale Carnegie, who forgot more than any of the rest of us ever knew about influencing others:

> People blunder through life trying to wig-wag other people into becoming interested in them. Of course, it doesn't work. People are not interested in you. They are interested in themselves—morning, noon, and after dinner.

YOU CAN BENEFIT FROM SHAWN'S EXPERIENCE

I can best demonstrate the power of focusing on your readers by telling you about my friend Shawn's recent adventure as a presenter.

Some colleagues and I were in Toronto, leading sales workshops for the middle managers of a large Internet security company. Early the first morning the participants entered the conference room, chatted with us in their friendly Canadian way, and took their seats. The last one in was Shawn, a young master of the universe, carrying a newspaper and eyeing the room for coffee. He poured a cup, found a seat at the back table, and noisily unfolded his newspaper while I opened the proceedings up front. Shawn was demonstrating that *he* was in charge of his time, not I.

Shawn continued perusing his paper for about five minutes, until the point where I must have said something interesting about how to prospect for sales, because he put the paper down and raised his hand. "Dennis," he said, "let me tell you what happened to me last week." I crossed my fingers and gave him the floor.

Shawn told us he had just come back from Victoria, British Columbia, where he represented his company at an industry conference. His team had rented a conference room just off the main floor, and had invited hundreds of prospects to come hear the pitch—25 people at a time. Shawn dutifully set up his laptop and projector and screen and called up a colorful Power-Point presentation.

"The first group filed in," Shawn said, "sat down around the table, and waited. I showed and told them all about my company for thirty minutes. I asked if there were any questions. There were none. They all thanked me politely and left. Odd, I thought. Maybe the next group will be better."

They weren't. The second group behaved exactly as the first group. No comments. No questions. Same for group three. Shawn was exasperated.

"Now I may look dumb," he told us, "but I'm not *that* dumb."

After lunch he put away his projector and laptop and simply smiled as the fourth group of the day marched in. When they were seated, Shawn introduced himself and his company and said, "Please tell me the top two concerns you have regarding security in your Web environment."

As he was relating the story to my group, Shawn got louder and more animated. "It was amazing!" he said. "They started talking to me and to each other and I couldn't get them to stop even when the hour was up. I finally sheep-dogged them out of the room and all the while they were throwing their business cards at me and begging me to call them to follow up. I'll never touch a laptop or a projector again."

I believe this is a profound lesson for all of us. Business professionals are consumed by their own problems and tasks. It is the rare individual who can stop thinking about himself long enough to really listen to you. Further, I believe we can apply that lesson directly to writing projects. I call it Chambers' First Law of Persuasion Dynamics:

> Writers persuade only to the degree that we talk about the reader's concerns.

Consider some of the reasons why this First Law works.

- It catches the reader's attention. You can't sell anything to anyone unless you first have that person's attention. People attend to what they care about. And what they care about is themselves.
- It positions you as an advocate for them. When they suddenly discover that you are talking about them and their needs, they begin to see you in a new light as someone who is on their side, and not just another vendor trying to sell them something.
- It uses a reader's innate self-directed interest as leverage to reduce that person's distrust. David Ogilvy, the late great advertising genius, said that "you cannot bore someone into buying your product." We bore people by talking about our product rather than their concerns. Similarly, you can't get them to award you the business unless they trust you. And they can't trust you unless you first get them to lower their suspicion. There's no better way to demonstrate your trustworthiness to disinterested readers than by showing them that you care more about them than you do about yourself and your company.

Here's another truth about proposals: Most business professionals hate them. First, they consume time and energy that may be better spent elsewhere. Second, all too often they go nowhere and result in a colossal waste of your resources. Third, losing pitch after pitch often leads to discouragement, and no one needs that. Fourth, writing them tends to take time away from actual clients who are paying the bills.

While all that is true, there are at least three benefits to writing powerful proposals that I hope you will consider.

- It's good business practice for you to write them. It keeps your skills sharp and helps maintain your business focus. Few dentists get visibly excited at the prospect of putting yet another cap on yet another tooth. But it's what they do.
- A proposal is the only way potentially to touch every decision-maker in your prospect's organization. In my career I have presented, in person, to over one hundred groups of clients and prospects. Invariably, when it comes time to ask for a decision, people in the meeting will say

something like, "Well, Sarah needs to decide on this and she's on the coast this week. Can you put something in writing and she'll get back to you?" So much for my dazzling personality. With a written proposal, you don't have to be there. People tend to circulate good proposals to everyone who matters.

- It is the only way to show the full range of your company's resources and abilities. In a presentation you have, say, up to twenty minutes before people start to check their electronic gadgets. A proposal, on the other hand, has a long shelf life. It contains every important element about your company and your relationship to the prospect. If they are interested, they will study your proposal for far longer than twenty minutes.

Of course, as mentioned, writing a proposal is often not optional. If you want the business, you have to write one.

CAVEAT: THERE IS ONE DOWNSIDE, AND IT IS POTENTIALLY HUGE

The company that asks for your solutions in a proposal could take your ideas and apply them without credit or remuneration. It happens rarely, but it does happen. Should you worry about it? Yes.

This is a constant fret among creative types in advertising agencies, to name just one industry. Prospective clients are always asking for ideas. They are looking for the one gonzo spot that will put their name on everyone's lips for a few days or weeks. However, most advertising ideas that catch fire in the public arena are pure serendipity. Nobody knows what will work until they put it out there and let the public decide. If advertising people knew for sure which idea would generate buzz before they published it, they would be really, really rich. The famous AFLAC duck is a case in point. Neither the agency nor the client had any idea that the entire world would begin imitating the quacking duck. But they thought the idea was good enough to give it a try. And it worked beyond anyone's dreams.

Concerning the theft of ideas, the most powerful factor in your favor is that every industry is a small world unto itself. The client who steals ideas is quickly labeled as a thief in the marketplace, and that tends to be self-policing.

The most egregious example I ran across recently was the case of a novice screenwriter in Boston who had what he thought was a good idea for a movie. He wrote it up in proper format and mailed it off to dozens of studios and producers. Years elapsed, and nothing came of his efforts. He moved on to other scripts and other work.

One evening he and his girlfriend decided to catch a movie that featured one of their favorite actors. As scene after scene unfolded, the screenwriter watched in increasing horror. It was his script. Some of the scenes were word for word as he had written them. As I'm writing this, the whole mess is in litigation. But so far he has received no apologies and no checks from anybody. "All I really want is a screen credit," he told one of the reporters for a Boston newspaper, "to establish my credentials for the next script I pitch."

He may wait a long time.

If you are worried about someone stealing your ideas, you have several recourses.

Most experienced screenwriters do one of the oldest tricks in the book: they mail a complete copy of their work to themselves. When it arrives, they file it but do not open it. The U.S. Postal Service will have stamped a date on the envelope. Every court in the land accepts the accuracy of this stamp as certifying the date, as long as the envelope is sealed.

You might do something similar. Mail a full copy of the proposal to yourself or your lawyer.

You might also stamp "PROPRIETARY" or "CONFIDENTIAL" on every page of your proposal. I don't recommend it, as it reminds your readers on every page that you don't trust them—not a good basis on which to begin a relationship.

You could indicate on your cover letter that the ideas and solutions supplied in the document are valuable and yours alone.

In any case, please talk with your attorney about your security concerns. They are worth worrying about.

9

Tie the Knot: Why Your Proposal Makes the Prospect so Nervous

> If you wish to persuade me, you must think my thoughts, feel my feelings, and speak my words.
>
> Cicero, Roman orator and statesman

Dictionary.com provides three definitions of a proposal:

1. The act of offering or suggesting something for acceptance, adoption, or performance.
2. A plan or scheme proposed.
3. An offer or suggestion of marriage.

That last one should scare you. You can be sure it scares the organization that issued the RFP. The executives on the issuing side know that they are just as likely to hire the wrong vendor as the right one. The world turns on its axis, and the marketing genius they thought they were awarding the proposal to turns out to be a fraud who knows how to cash checks. So they will look for anything in your proposal that will give them the slightest reason to turn you down. As any lawyer will tell you, it is far safer to say no than yes. To say yes to you means they are saying no to everyone else and now trust their lucky stars that they made the right decision. That's why, for example, so many senior executive and governmental positions are going unfilled these days. "No" is safer than "yes."

I once worked in a large advertising agency that hired a new executive creative director, imported from one of the biggest agencies in the world. The guy's portfolio was so good, we were surprised his old agency was willing to let him go. My agency looked to him to be a rainmaker and profit builder. The man's first act was to fire three senior creative people. His next act was to fire several of the Hollywood production studios with whom the agency had built relationships over many years; this genius preferred higher-priced London studios. His third act was to retreat to his office and come up with a dozen of the worst advertising ideas I have personally ever seen and insist that we present them to our clients. Over a period of six months he alienated two of our biggest clients and drove out a handful of our most experienced art directors and copywriters. After nine months, he was fired. The agency never recovered from such a walking disaster. We certainly should have said no to him at the beginning. But in the beginning, people tend to be in love.

Which brings me to marriage.

For a company to bring in any big-ticket vendor such as you to work closely with them is tantamount to marriage. For better or worse, your futures are now linked. And as in any human marriage, getting hitched is easy; getting divorced is expensive. If you wonder why so many issuers of RFPs are so darned picky, that's why. They know their economic future is on the line.

So before we take up the question of how to convince them to marry you, let's discuss whether you really want to marry them.

When you compete for big projects, a formal proposal is likely to be the primary basis on which you are selected—or rejected. Your first question ought to be: Should we devote the time and energy it will take to write a proposal (or create a pitch or work out a bid) for this prospect?

THE YES OR NO CHECKLIST

Please check any that apply to your situation. If you check more than half, I suggest that you consider the RFP to be a long shot.

___ The prospect has never heard of us.
___ We know nothing about the prospect.
___ We have had no business dealings with this prospect.
___ Our sales force has never contacted this prospect for any reason.
___ The prospect's problem or need is not clear in the RFP.
___ They are looking for an outcome that is beyond the reach of our expertise.
___ If we win the account, we will have to hire new personnel.
___ The RFP is a conglomeration of boilerplate-style paragraphs.
___ The issuer forbids us to contact them for any reason.
___ The issuer is looking not just for proof of our competence, but for specific solutions.
___ Writing this proposal will take several of our senior people offline for at least two weeks.
___ The prospect has issued more than twenty RFPs for this particular project.
___ The RFP is confusing or poorly written.
___ Fulfilling the RFP will cost us more than 5 percent of our monthly revenue.

Sometimes turning down an RFP for which you would be an inappropriate choice takes more courage than simply writing a proposal. The siren song of a new account—any new account—is hard to resist. Only you and your team can make that decision. If you already have a policy in place regarding which RFPs you will answer and which you will not, then you are ahead of the game. If you have no written policy regarding RFPs, this may be the best time to create one. The exercise is well worth the time.

Let's say, however, that after due consideration, you and your team decide that this is an account you want to pursue with all guns blazing. Good. In that case, put your best people on the project, and give them the time and money to do it right. This is likely to cause you and your organization some pain. Good. All worthwhile relationships cause some pain, at least in the beginning. When one gets married to a person, one "forsakes all others." Good. That kind of pain means you are serious. If you go after this account and win it, your enterprise will have to do a little forsaking, too. If you work with A, you can't work with B. If you are ready for that kind of relationship with A, then you're ready to win.

TEN COMMANDMENTS FOR WRITING A KILLER PROPOSAL

I'll list all ten (with apologies to Moses), then we'll take a look at them.

One. No boilerplate. Not even one paragraph.

Two. Begin with the assurance of compliance.

Three. Describe in your own words, not the language of the RFP, the exact outcome that the prospect is seeking in vocabulary the prospect understands.

Four. Deal with the money up front.

Five. Avoid writing about your company for ten pages longer than you can stand it.

Six. Follow all my rules for twenty-first century grammar and punctuation.

Seven. Let one writer create the entire first draft, and let it be original to this project.

Eight. Avoid all clichés.

Nine. Create a Work Breakdown Structure or a Gantt chart for your proposal project.

Ten. Do not delegate a proposal to junior people.

One. No Boilerplate. Not Even One Paragraph

Boilerplate was not invented to be read. It exists for one reason—to cover one's vulnerabilities in the event of problems. It is a legal necessity, or so the lawyers tell us. Perhaps. But boilerplate has gotten out of hand. Some television and radio commercials end with the idiotic hyperspeed reading of legalese that is not meant to be understood. It is meant to be *there*, in the event that some hapless consumer spends too much or eats too much or sues too much. When that happens, the lawyers in court simply point to the boilerplate and declare, "See, your honor, it is there. It was there all the time."

Boilerplate can sabotage your proposal. All the inferences a reader can possibly make from it are negative:

- You don't trust me.
- You don't care enough about me to put this in regular English.
- You don't care enough about me to take the time to write it so I can understand it.
- You are submitting fifteen proposals this week, and this boilerplate junk is saving you time.
- This is a mere copy of a proposal you sent to someone else—probably a competitor of ours—last week.
- You are putting escape clauses in the fine print.
- Boilerplate is always about you.
- You don't really want my business.

The object of a proposal is to sell something: your service, your product, your creativity, your technical expertise, your company as a working partner, and so on. Boilerplate cannot do that. It is so negative, so off-putting, that I recommend you avoid it altogether. Write an original proposal every time, or else don't bother. The issuer is looking for a unique solution to a problem; boilerplate, by its very nature, is not unique. It is a killer.

I'm not suggesting that you have to reinvent the wheel every time. Do what professional writers do: Keep a storyline framework that you like and write inside that frame. Don't use the same words every time, but follow the framework. For example, AIDA may be the most common framework among direct-response copywriters:

- Attention
- Interest
- Desire
- Action

You can't do anything without first grabbing the reader's attention. Whether it's a sentence from left field or a stunning promise or whatever—get the attention.

You attract interest by talking about them.

You generate desire by making what you have to offer as appealing and popular as possible.

And you drive to action with the simplest possible way to get back to you.

Another one I have used from time to time is the Four Ps: Promise, Picture, Proof, Push.

You can go classic with Beginning, Middle, End.

You can create one for yourself that has lots of energy for you. The one I use often I created long ago: Main Headline, Illustration, Illustration, Secondary Headline, Illustration, Appeal to Authority, Testimonials, Call to Action.

Whatever framework you use, remember Dr. Johnson's sage advice: "Promise, large promise, is the soul of an advertisement." Your proposal is a piece of sales writing, an advertisement for your company, so make sure you are early with that large promise.

Two. Begin with the Assurance of Compliance

People issue RFPs in order to compare responses and vendors. You are taking advantage of this desire if you put a graphic that demonstrates your compliance with the RFP as near the front as possible (after the cover letter and other essentials). A compliance graphic demonstrates visually and impactfully how what you are offering matches with what the issuer needs. It is the fastest way possible for you to assure readers that—first—you understand exactly what they are looking for and—second—that you can provide it.

SAMPLE OF COMPLIANCE GRAPHIC

How the products and services of Raisbeck Equestrian Supply comply with the requirements of Nevada State Rodeo, Inc.

Requirement	Compliance	Page	Remarks
Just-in-time delivery of 750 lbs of oats and two tons hay per day for five days.	Full	14	This will eliminate storage and security expenses for NSRI while assuring freshness. Delivery by 05:30 each day.
Maintenance and repair services of tack, ropes, all relevant equipment.	Full	18	RES has a full tack workshop in Smith Valley, plus a fully equipped 14-ft trailer for on-site repairs. The proprietor is a licensed tack repairman.
Blacksmith and farrier services 24 hours per day.	Partial	21	If awarded the contract, we will subcontract with Cowart Farrier Inc, of Reno for full 24-hour services.
Qualified repair technician from RES on standby for entire length of rodeo.	Full	23	

And so on. This is just a quick homemade sample. A thorough compliance graphic with quick hits on your main strengths is a professional way to show at a glance all of the advantages that working with you will bring to the issuer.

Three. Describe in Your Own Words, Not the Language of the RFP, the Exact Outcome That the Prospect Is Seeking in Vocabulary the Prospect Understands

Repeating the issuing company's words back to them has no value. A better response is to describe their challenges from your perspective using non-jargon vocabulary. The point of this is the same point you have in writing the entire proposal: to *persuade*.

How are human beings persuaded? Dictionaries tell us that persuasion is a kind of influence, a means of guiding others to see it our way without using force. Armies, police officers, and the IRS do not have to waste time persuading people to do anything—they can use force. Presidential candidates, sellers of cereal, and business professionals cannot use force—we must persuade. In my research I have learned that nobody really knows a foolproof method of persuasion that works every time—but we know what tends to work.

You are likely to persuade people if you can convince them that you are thinking and working on their behalf, not yours.

Last year my wife and I bought a circa-1800 brick federal-style house in a New England town famous for its colonial and Victorian homes. Our plan was to rehabilitate the first floor from two aging apartments to a gleaming retro flat for ourselves. We invited three contractors in the area to bid on the project.

The first builder was strictly A-list, the big kahuna. He came in with a soup-to-nuts proposal that was stunning in its breadth. And in its price tag. But I knew I would be uncomfortable in the space that he would provide, just as I always am in the back of a limo. It was too marvelous.

The second bidder was a good guy, good reputation, but he came in with a proposal for the home he would like to live in. It wasn't us.

The third one was the charm. He listened to us. How did we like to live during the week? What did we like to do on weekends? Wood or gas fireplace? What kind of art did we like? What was our time frame? Do we have frequent overnight guests? What was our budget? And so on. We went with him, because he would build us the home we wanted to live in, not the home he wanted to live in. We found his focus on us to be ... *persuasive*. It was that focus that made us reach for the checkbook.

If you think back to a time when you bought a big-ticket item, like a car or house or thoroughbred racehorse, what was the persuasion factor that tipped you over? It's an exercise well worth doing. I suspect that in almost every case you were able to see yourself using that item. If a salesperson was involved, it was probably someone smart enough to keep out of the way and let you sell yourself on the purchase. Similarly, you want to get your readers to see themselves using you and your company to build their own profits.

I'll bring up the topic of persuasion again in a later chapter.

Four. Deal with the Investment Up Front

I live hard by the Atlantic Ocean and a stone's throw from the Maine state line. With those icy Maine waters so close, we have lobster often. We also have blizzards often—it's a kind of natural balance. In these parts there are two kinds of dinner guests: the kind who eat the lobster tail first and the kind who save it for last. The tail is the lobster's finest gift to humanity. Those who eat it first are thinking, "While my taste buds are fresh and bursting with eagerness, I'll bite into that lobster tail and die of pleasure." The lobster-tail-last people are thinking, "I'll enjoy the whole meal more while anticipating the joy to come of dipping the final bite of lobster tail into the dish of melted and salted butter." (Sorry, I get carried away thinking of lobster.)

Similarly, the world of proposal writers is divided into Money Early and Money Late types. I advocate Money Early, because that's probably the number-one issue your reader cares about. If you've ever spent days preparing a proposal, only to see your readers quickly flip through your cleanly wrought prose to discover how much money this is going to set them back, you know what I mean.

Why not give it to them the way they want it? They will do it their way regardless of how you organize the material. And by easing their concern up front about money, they may be more likely to follow the thread of your arguments and end up seeing things your way.

If you are making a presentation in person, then I recommend that you talk about the investment near the end because you can make a good case for it. No one, you hope, will be so rude as to interrupt you. But in writing they will simply go there first.

The best way I've found to deal with the whole "how much will this baby cost me" issue is to embed the finances within a discussion of what outcomes the prospect is seeking. The richer the outcomes, the more likely your prospects are to appreciate the expertise you bring to the party. And expertise is expensive.

While we're on the subject, you might want to consider the universe of outcomes. Being able to put yourself in the prospect's shoes and think about the outcomes that will make him or her a superstar is a skill that takes lots of practice. Developing that skill has the further benefit of helping you to see it from the client's point of view faster and automatically.

For example, Unilever, the producers of Surf, were facing this very challenge a few decades ago when they came out with their new laundry detergent product in a fiercely competitive environment that included Tide and Cheer. The big boys were trumpeting *Brighter than Bright!* and *Whiter than White!* to homemakers who seemingly put on sunglasses every time they did a load of wash. The lab people at Surf were not convinced that white and bright were the outcomes that people wanted when they washed clothes.

So the researchers did what all business people should do: they observed their customers using the product in their natural habitat. They sat for countless hours in laundromats across the land. They immediately observed a curious thing. People who did lots of laundry seemed to care little or not at all about brightness or whiteness. How did real people determine whether their load of laundry was clean? You know the answer—they smelled it. Put their noses right up against the fabrics and sniffed. Eureka! Surf added more scent to their detergent than the competitors and a new brand was launched with a bang. The outcome people really wanted for their freshly washed laundry was that it smelled nice. How easy was that?

It was so easy that the people who had been flogging *whiter* and *brighter* put a range of scents in their detergents immediately after Surf did so, and they too watched their sales rise. There are many lessons here, not the least of which is that your competitors will do exactly what you do, if it works. It's your job, then, to be the first one to do it.

In every meeting I have with every new prospect, I am careful to find out exactly what outcome(s) they are looking for. And if nothing else, I give them that or I give them their money back.

Linda Thaler and Robin Koval, in their book *Bang! Getting Your Message Heard in a Noisy World*, emphasize this same point while discussing their most famous account, AFLAC insurance. The CEO on the client side came to their ad agency with one request: Get the average consumer to remember our name. It's a compelling story of a simple request that the ad executives were smart enough to heed. In the end, they came up with a classic ad campaign because they were focused on doing that one thing. AFLAC spoken aloud sounds like a duck's quack. So it was a matter of getting the duck in situations where he had to say AFLAC a dozen times in a thirty-second commercial. And they made the CEO happy while making themselves prosperous.

(In one of their award-winning spots in the series, the duck is trumpeting the AFLAC name in an auto repair shop. Every time the duck quacks the name, a noise from some outside source like a truck horn or a blast from an air compressor overrides the duck. So I found myself filling in the name for him. Here I am, a potential customer, watching the commercial and saying "AFLAC" out loud to myself. I was too impressed with the sheer genius of it all to be embarrassed.)

I've had clients answer the question about outcomes in a wide range of ways, from "I want to increase my brand's market share by two points" to "I want our beer to be the sexy beer." One client actually told me, "What I really want is for my golf buddies on Saturday morning to tell me they saw my commercial and thought it was clever." So I gave him a clever television spot that had little impact on sales, and he was happy anyway. Give them what they want in your proposal. Whatever they want for an outcome, give it to them if you can. Those few times that I ignored the outcomes that the clients wanted because I had a better idea—I ended up regretting it.

One final tip: The only outcomes that really matter are those that you can measure. My golfing client could measure the number of buddies who told him they saw and liked the spot. If it isn't measurable, you'll never know how close you came to fulfilling the request. If you can measure the outcome, you can measure your success.

Here are some typical outcomes. I suggest you start making a list, and keep building it to remind yourself that prospects want outcomes.

Business Outcomes

- Increase market share
- Reduce turnover
- Reduce absenteeism
- Improve training for new hires
- Increase sales
- Deal with fewer returns of unsatisfactory merchandise
- Improve return on investment
- Help leverage more data
- Improve maintenance records
- Redesign processes

Technical Outcomes

- Reduce the learning curve
- Improve scalability
- Remove bugs
- Increase automation
- Enhance Web security
- Improve click-throughs
- Enlarge data storage
- Make data more accessible

Customer Outcomes

- Enhance brand awareness
- Update packaging
- Increase satisfaction
- Reduce help-desk queues
- Increase efficiencies to help lower prices
- Answer phones faster

Five. Avoid Writing about Your Company for Ten Pages Longer Than You Can Stand It

Clearly you cannot focus entirely on the issuer's needs. At some point you will need to discuss your company and the ways you can help. That's fine. But put it off for one more page. Then another. Keep talking about them. This will be hard, but it will make you successful. You should keep putting it off because once you start writing about how wonderful your company is, you won't be able to stop. Why? Because this is the center of your comfort zone. This is what you love to talk about. More than one proposal writer has written herself out of the winner's circle.

Consider our old friend Aristotle. He wrote several books on rhetoric, which he defined as "seeing the available means of persuasion in any given situation." We can learn from him. The wise student of Aristotle will not ask, "How can we sell our products or services to these guys?" Instead, he will ask, "What do they really want? Let's find out, and do our best to give it to them." If this sounds elementary to you, it is. The only reason I dare to mention it is that few business professionals ever do it.

Six. Follow My Rules for Twenty-First Century Grammar and Punctuation

This is a new century loaded with new technology. Yet many business people still write as if this were the age of manual typewriters. (If you are under thirty, please Google "typewriter" and look at pictures of them if you want a good laugh.) An example: Many business writers tap out two spaces after a period to begin the next sentence. That practice comes from the old IBM "Selectric" days, when writers hammered on a little ball that contained all the letters. Each letter was given the same spacing. A capital I was given the same space as a capital M. So to even out the look on the page, people tapped two spaces before beginning a new sentence. Modern software makes that action obsolete, by quietly moving letters together for a balanced look. It's a new day.

Similarly, text messaging and e-mail and blogging have reshaped our rules of grammar and punctuation to suit the new technical realities. I can't say I like all of the changes, but who am I to blow against the wind?

I discuss some of the more important new grammar and punctuation rules in Chapter 7.

One aspect of writing that hasn't changed is that high-level readers expect no errors. This is not fair. Many unusually bright people can't seem to remember when to use a comma and when to use a semicolon. Should they be punished for that? No, but they are. Grammar and punctuation errors imply to readers that the writer is either not serious or not well educated. It is the way things are.

Every four years Americans gather like global villagers around the television to hear the various candidates for president debate each other. Many of us vote for a candidate based on his or her ability to function well in an artificial debate situation. The moderator asks a question, and the candidates respond. We judge the responses, give them time to have at each other politely, and then decide who won. We tend to vote accordingly. This is not fair, but we do it. Once elected, the president will never debate anyone in a stand-up format like this. He or she will consult with advisers and issue written statements or deliver carefully wrought speeches. He or she will not debate anyone on live television ever again. Yet this is how we like to elect our politicians.

Similarly, how well or poorly you fare in a written proposal suggests to the client how well or poorly you will fare in a business relationship. If your writing mechanics are unsatisfactory, you won't have a chance.

Seven. Let One Writer Create the Entire First Draft, and Let It Be Original to This Project

Committees make poor writers.

Have you ever participated in a committee that was trying to write something, even something small such as a press statement? Group dynamics take over. People jockey to show their skills. Fresh, creative ideas die a quick death, while overused language rises to the fore. It is the triumph of the lowest common denominator. People in groups tire quickly, and so they all rush to write down something they can live with and move on.

"I can live with it" is not the standard for good writing.

Even a triumph of committee writing, such as the U. S. Constitution, was written by two or three people and then discussed by many more. Typically one person is inspired to send a proposal to a certain prospect. Let that one person write the first draft. If you have a capable writer on staff, someone with knowledge of writing mechanics and who can function as an editor, let her have the second look to edit. Then let everyone who is entitled to comment on the draft send their recommended changes to that editor. Let the editor and the originator of the first draft work to include all other worthy ideas. And finally let the originator finalize and smooth out the proposal so that it has one voice and one style.

Eight. Avoid All Clichés

Clichés, like boilerplate, are credibility killers. They tell your readers that you simply don't care enough about the project to write in a fresh style.

Here are some of the clichés that I see every day:

- In the event that …
- Please be advised …
- At that point in time …
- Enclosed please find …
- Please do not hesitate to call …

And the cliché of the year: Think outside the box …

There are several websites devoted to examining and listing clichés—a quick look at them will help you to see why some of your favorite expressions should be abandoned now.

Nine. Create a Work Breakdown Structure or a Gantt Chart for Your Proposal Project

Let's say that you are the original writer for a new proposal to a new prospect. I suggest getting all interested parties around a conference table and brainstorming for twenty to thirty minutes on several important concepts:

- What does this prospect want or need from us as a vendor?
- Is this the prospect's real problem? If so, is it worth our addressing? If not, what is the real problem?
- Can we solve or help to solve their real problem?
- What applications or products or services do we have that will solve their real problem?
- If they adapt and follow our recommendations, what are the results likely to be?
- What is the full scope of our investment in gathering the information and writing this proposal?
- Why should they choose us rather than some other vendor?

Once you are clear about what you have to offer, then decide who is going to provide what input—and when. The best tools I know of for this task are a Work Breakdown Structure (WBS) and a Gantt chart. (Chapter 4 has an example of a Gantt chart.)

The point of a WBS is to ensure that all the necessary tasks are written down and that someone is assigned to do them. Do not assign calendar dates to these tasks yet. That's what a Gantt chart is for. Also note that each column is self-contained and does not rely on any other column.

A Gantt chart puts the WBS tasks in proper order and schedules them. The true beauty of a Gantt chart is that one can see at a glance just how on or off schedule the project is.

Ten. Do Not Delegate a Proposal to Junior People

Let me expand on this idea just a bit in order to make it crystal clear: Do not delegate a proposal to junior people.

And that's it. Ten steps to getting the work that'll keep the company going and put food on the table. One last thing: Most RFPs dictate an outline. Follow it to the letter. You'd be amazed how many first-line decision-makers (especially in the government) will bounce your proposal for not following their outline.

10

The Art and Science of Persuasion: Convince Readers to See It Your Way

If things seem under control, you're just not going fast enough.
Mario Andretti, Racecar Driver

Back in 1957 (during the dark early days of the Cold War) Vance Packard wrote a best-selling book titled *The Hidden Persuaders*. It was his premise that those wicked advertising people used subliminal tricks like a buried message in one or two frames of film to speak directly to consumers' subconscious minds and force them to buy things they didn't need. Even worse, some villainous art directors (he claimed) buried satanic or sexual images in ice cubes to attract the reader's subconscious libido and entice readers to act on those forbidden urges. As an advertising practitioner for many years, I can tell you this: We're not that smart. I can also promise you this: If we knew how to do it, we would. If I knew how to compel you without force to buy a Cadillac rather than a Lexus, I would. If I could effortlessly and legally compel you in an advertisement to buy a Braun blender rather than a Waring blender, I would, and I'd feel guilty about it over champagne cocktails aboard my yacht.

The simple truth is that nobody knows how to persuade every time. We know what works in volume—the direct-response industry is built on it. But we don't know how to persuade individuals with certainty every time.

Sherlock Holmes used unassailable logic based on observation to persuade his clients that he had learned the truth. Stephen Hawking uses mathematics or calculus or quantum physics (who knows?) to persuade his readers that his theories about black holes are correct. Advertising people use sexual images, or discount pricing, or simple begging. Sales representatives practice good body language and use a well-tended day planner. College professors use the threat of a poor grade. Sports agents use the economic principle of scarcity: There's only one Tiger Woods. We all use something to persuade others to see things our own particular way.

If you are using proposal writing to persuade prospects that you and your company are their best choice, here is what seems to work often:

- Study the RFP, and reconstruct in your opening paragraph the problem or challenge or need that the issuer has in your own words and based on your own understanding.
- Clearly list the outcomes that the prospect needs or is looking for.
- Suggest that you have the best solution, using as many specifics as you can.

What this procedure has going for it is that you begin your pitch talking about them, not about you.

Our modern understanding of persuasion is built on the two foundations of art and science. Persuasion is an art because successful practitioners of it use feelings to get people to take the action the persuader favors. It is a science because it can be quantified as certain behaviors that seem to be hard-wired in the brain.

One early proponent of this idea was M. W. Fox, a prolific researcher in the field of animal behavior. One of his famous experiments involved a mother turkey, among the most protective and nurturing mothers in the animal kingdom. All of a mother turkey's maternal instincts seem to be triggered by the plaintive *cheep cheep cheep* of turkey chicks. When a mother turkey hears that sound, she nurtures the originator. No sound, no nurturing. This makes a kind of brutal sense. If a chick is too weak to make a sound, the mother is wise not to waste food on it and to favor the healthy, sound-producing chicks.

In the experiment, Fox used a string to pull a stuffed polecat—a turkey's natural foe—into the turkey's field of vision. The mama turkey instantly attacked the hapless polecat with talons and beak. But when Fox pulled the same stuffed polecat into range a second time it contained a small tape recorder that played the *cheep cheep* sound of a chick. This time the mother turkey gathered the polecat beneath her wings. A polecat!

One sees this kind of behavior among animals often. It is called a *fixed-action pattern*, according to Robert B. Cialdini, one of the leading researchers on the nature of persuasion. (His most recent book is *Influence: Science and Practice*.) We should realize two things, he says, about them.

First, the automatic, fixed-action patterns of these animals work very well most of the time. For example, because only normal, healthy turkey chicks make the peculiar sound of baby turkeys, it makes sense for mother turkeys to respond maternally to that single cheep-cheep noise. By reacting to just that one stimulus, the average mother turkey will nearly always behave correctly. It takes a trickster like a scientist to make her tapelike response seem silly. The second important thing to understand is that we, too, have our preprogrammed tapes; and although they usually work to our advantage, the trigger features that activate them can dupe us into playing the tapes at the wrong times.

This is where the overwhelming data flow of modern life comes into play for the savvy proposer. Where there is too much information, most people look to an expert to make their decisions for them. If you and your company are seen by the prospect as experts, with the prospect's needs in mind, you have a strong likelihood of winning the account.

According to Cialdini, influencing others to exhibit the behaviors you want takes several sophisticated forms.

- Reciprocation. Someone gives you something for free; you tend to reciprocate in kind. There's a reason your server in a restaurant includes a few mints with your bill: It increases the tip. So if, for example, your proposal includes a separate package of a free White Paper on a topic of interest with useful, relevant information, your prospect will be more inclined to see you as an expert and a source of helpful knowledge.
- Commitment and Consistency. "Once we make a choice or take a stand," he says, "we will encounter personal and interpersonal pressures to behave consistently with that commitment." Other authorities suggest that when it comes to making decisions on something as complex as a written business proposal, readers make up their minds within a matter of minutes. So if they decide in your favor early on, they are simply looking for arguments from you to justify their decision. If they decide against you early on, there is little you can say later that will turn them around. The lesson: Convince them early in the proposal that you are the best choice—don't wait until page 14 to really hammer them with great ideas.
- Social Proof. "We view a behavior as correct in a given situation," Cialdini says, "to the degree that we see others performing it." If you can bolster your company as the best choice with glowing testimonials or with names and phone numbers of other clients who love your services, you'll be giving yourself a good chance to win, especially with prospects who are not that familiar with you.

THE PRICE HAS TO BE RIGHT

In proposals the issue of pricing comes up as perhaps the most sensitive of all. You don't want to price yourself out of contention with a bid twice as high as anyone else. Nor do you want to be the lowball bidder who seems not to have understood the RFP.

Pricing as a form of persuasion in sales has only recently come under study. This anecdotal evidence tends to suggest that the road to riches has two lanes: high and low. The vast middle is a no-man's-land where few can make a profit. The retailers who are flourishing these days in a fierce competitive landscape are those who occupy the elite end and the low-price end. The Tiffanys and Wal-Marts among us are doing well; the middle-roaders are struggling.

In the 1970s, a well-known work-boot manufacturer engaged a small Boston advertising agency to help increase sales. The boot maker was in danger of drowning in red ink. Their product was perceived as low end, and retail staffers in local shoe stores turned up their noses at the orange boots as ugly and merely for "blue collar" working types. In fact, the boots were well made: The leather was good quality and the manufacturing process was time-tested. Even so, the boots seemed glued to the shelves.

The agency principals came up with a piece of advice that made marketing history and increased the agency's size tenfold almost overnight. The advice was counter-intuitive but spot on: Double the price of the boots.

The clients were staggered by the idea. But nobody's buying them now! What about a wide-ranging print campaign? What about radio?

No, the agency people said. That comes later. For now, double the price and do nothing else.

The client did, reluctantly. Within weeks, sales doubled. Within months, stores were making emergency calls to the manufacturer that they were out of stock and when could they get more? The entire Boston area was aflame with desire for those boots. It was a lesson that few retailers have ignored since. People don't want the lowest-priced goods. They want a bargain. They want high-quality goods, on sale.

Your bid in your proposal should reflect that truth. You want to be awarded the account, and you want to make a profit. You can have both happen, if you focus entirely on the needs and issues of the prospect.

THE FIRST PERSON IN AMERICA TO BUY A TROOPER II

Back in the early 1980s I was in the market for a new car. My wife and I had two young children, and needed something with room that didn't remind everyone of my dad's station wagon. As it happened, the Isuzu Trooper II had just come into showrooms. I saw one while I was driving home one evening, and stopped for a look-see. It was late. The manager himself was the only one minding the store. He came out, introduced himself, chuckled at the way the Trooper looked like a box on wheels, told me he just got this one vehicle that morning and hadn't even been inside it himself, and asked if I wanted to take it for a spin.

I did. He tucked into the passenger seat, and off we went. He casually asked me all about myself, never once mentioning the car. What sports did I like? What did I do on weekends? How old were my children? What did they like to do? What was my dream vacation? And on and on. He got the whole family story. I heard not one word about the Trooper because I was too busy talking about myself.

Back at the dealership, we got out and I kicked the tires. "You know, Dennis," the manager said, patting the warm hood gently and seeming to notice the car for the first time, "you could hunt rhinos in this thing."

"I'll take it," I said.

I remember him fondly as the world's greatest salesman. He focused on me, not on his product. And when it was time to close the deal, he knew exactly the words to say that would help me make the sale for him. I never did hunt rhinos in that car, but I always knew I could.

YOUR SUCCESS IN YOUR PROPOSAL—AND IN THE LIFE OF YOUR COMPANY—DEPENDS ON HOW THE CUSTOMER FEELS ABOUT YOU

Among the things that puzzle me in this brave new world of ours are gas stations. I remember when an attendant at any gas station in America would be glad to check your oil, gauge your tires, and clean your windshield for free. It sounds quaint and even a little silly now to write such a thing, but it's true. So when and why did everything change? When did every last gas station on the planet decide that they were doing us a favor to let us drive up, pump our own gas, and drive away without so much as a friendly wave from the owner?

Isn't there one gas station owner out there who thinks to grab an edge over his competitors by being just a tiny bit friendly? I go to the station two blocks from my house. I've been doing it for years. The owner wouldn't recognize me if I plowed into his air pump (for which he changes me fifty cents for one minute's worth of air). And I would drop him instantly for any gas station that treated me just a little better.

In this modern age, I believe that the company that builds relationships with its customers builds business. Think about your own experience. Is there a company or service provider that you have remained loyal to, possibly even when it was inconvenient? I'm sure the answer is yes.

I hate to change banks. It is a supreme headache to get new checks, new account numbers, new ATM cards, new everything. And so I stay with my bank as long as I can. But I have left one bank for another on occasion, and it always had to do with my growing sense that they didn't care whether I stayed or went somewhere else.

Earning a customer's loyalty is relatively easy, but you have to keep earning it. The moment you stop earning it, they start thinking about the greener grass next door.

Some years back I visited my brother in Minneapolis on the way home from a long road trip. I needed to pick up some little gifts for my wife and daughters, as was my custom after a few weeks away, so we went to the storied Mall of America, the largest shopping mall on earth. I had in mind to spend about $30, and some nice soap or shampoo seemed like a good idea. We found an upscale little soap shop and met Anne, a remarkable relationship builder. Evidently our walking into the place had made her day. She took us on a wondrous tour of the store, where every item seemed more enchanting than the last. She asked about my daughters' names and ages, my wife's preferences for perfumes, and my own feelings about citrus-based shampoos (turns out I'm for them). We had a grand time, and responded with our credit cards. I bought nearly $200 worth of soap and my brother bought just a little less. Anne wrapped each purchase separately with a note for each recipient. It was my best retail experience ever.

At home, recovered from the elation, I wrote a letter to Anne's boss at the shop, telling her of my grand experience under Anne's tutelage and recommending that whatever she was paying Anne to double it.

No response from the boss. But two months later I got a letter from Anne, thanking me for my letter. It seems the boss ignored my recommendation, and so Anne took my letter to Nordstrom and got hired at twice her old salary. Relationship is everything.

SPEAKING OF NORDSTROM ...

You have heard of Nordstrom, no matter where you live. What have you heard? They're the customer service people. Legends abound about Nordstrom people going the extra mile for customers. There's the shoe clerk who met a customer at the airport with a replacement pair of shoes. There's the customer who demanded and got her money back for a set of tires she wasn't happy with. (Nordstrom doesn't sell tires.) There's the customer who needed a suit altered that very afternoon or else he wouldn't buy it, and so they brought in a tailor from another store. Hey, wait a minute, that was me.

Customer service is all there is. Products are a too-delicate platform on which to build a company. If you hit the market with an innovative, life-changing product, someone will copy it and sell it at a lower price before the ink is dry on your new logo. Technology changes rapidly, often not in your favor. Ask the guy who sold the world's finest buggy whips on the day that Mr. Ford rolled out his first mass-production car. Ask Wang. Ask Polaroid. Of course you need products and services. But customers can get them from any number of providers, often at a price lower than yours.

When you build your company on relationships, on service, on caring about the people who buy from you, it will last. If your commitment to relationship shines through in your proposal, you have given yourself and your organization the best chance to win.

11

Watch Winners at Work: A Model Proposal

My only day off is the day I pitch.
Roger Clemens, Cy Young Award-winning pitcher,
on his workout ethic

This is an actual, successful proposal created by Mr. Len D'Innocenzo, the CEO of CRKInteractive, an organization dedicated to classroom and online training in the areas of corporate sales, leadership, and customer service. Mr. D'Innocenzo is an author, entrepreneur, and sales expert. I am grateful for his permission to use one of his proposals as an example for my readers.

As you will see, Len D'Innocenzo walks the walk. Before he writes the proposal, he applies his "Facts Issues Needs Dreams" interview format while discussing projects with prospects. He does this because he wants to find out how the prospect will measure the value of his proposal. And because he knows that any winning proposal is all about them—not about him or his company. "It's one of the reasons we win most of the proposals we submit," he told me recently.

In this case, the prospect is an international, high-tech, sales-based organization whose aim with the RFP was to find a sales-training company that could offer both classroom and online workshops for both new hires and veterans.

The proposal you see is about half of its original length. I have kept all of the core thinking. If you contact Mr. D'Innocenzo at www.crkinteractive.com, I'm sure he will be glad to share the original with you. I have changed or edited out any proprietary information; all the financial information that remains is entirely fictional. I wanted readers mainly to see the value and strength of a proposal that is focused on the reader.

It begins with a strong cover letter, suggesting to the client that this proposal will be all about his needs, not CRKI's background. The Table of Contents underscores the emphasis on the client. And the body of the proposal is relentlessly focused on the client's critical needs and CRKI's proposed solution to meet those needs. Where most proposal writers focus on their strengths, D'Innocenzo focuses on the client's needs and the satisfaction the client will feel when those needs are successfully met.

If any errors remain, they are entirely mine.

[Cover Letter]
January 14, 20XX

Mr. Charles Rainier
CEO, Merrimac River Enterprises
123 State Street
Middletown OH 12345

Dear Mr. Rainier:

Thank you for providing us with the information to prepare this proposal. From the input we have received from both you and Mark Pfaff, you have clearly thought through every aspect of your sales challenges and the solutions required. We are convinced you have identified all of your challenges correctly and are glad to respond.

Our recommendations and investment are detailed in the attached proposal.

Bottom line: The program we are recommending will achieve all of your desired goals and objectives. It will have additional benefits that will accrue to you at no cost, and we detail those in the proposal.

You identified three areas in which we should concentrate the training efforts:

1. Increase sales productivity to grow MRE's core business and maintain a strong financial model.
2. Expand MRE's existing customer base by fine-tuning and adapting the sales training to meet the different development needs of the regional direct teams, channel account managers, and business development teams.
3. Enhance managers' leadership ability to become sales coaches who develop their teams to identify and solve customers' emerging points of pain.

We can be of significant value to you in all three areas. Further, we add value with basic sales "blocking & tackling" fundamentals that support your objectives. These fundamentals include

- Adjusting selling styles to match customer behavioral styles
- Building stronger and longer lasting relationships with clients
- Successfully shifting from "product-focused" to "solution-focused" selling
- Gaining higher levels of repeat business from existing or dormant accounts.

We look forward to working with you on this important initiative.

Sincerely yours,
Len D'Innocenzo

TABLE OF CONTENTS

Client Needs and Solution

Needed

A modular sales development system for MRE's sales organization that will produce the following measurable results over the short and long term:

1. Enhance the professional sales skills of the organization.
2. Articulate how MRE's value proposition aligns to customer's strategic business objectives.
3. Establish a comprehensive sales process to leverage previous success, qualify new opportunities, and sell the value of doing business with MRE.
4. Help the management team to coach and successfully implement the "common" sales process to achieve the above results.
5. Minimize costs and lost selling time in delivery of these workshops while achieving the desired results.

Solution

The MRE sales training solution is a customized solution with the option to utilize a blended learning approach. Content will be based on MRE's specific business needs and will incorporate components of CRKInteractive's "Customer Focused Selling" and "21st Century Leadership" series.

We will provide an easy-to-use process that sales people can incorporate into their daily activities and managers can reinforce through coaching. Customer Focused Selling will raise the performance level of the entire organization to reflect the best practices of top performers. Participants will quickly unlock their potential for more sales, higher profits, and improved ROI.

Critical Factors for Success

1. *Target Audience*

   • Sales Team & Management Team (approximately 400 people)

2. *Sales Team Solution Format*

PHASE I—July Sales Meeting: Kickoff Customer-Focused Selling

   • $1/2$ Day of Classroom training
   • Behavior Styles and Selling Styles

PHASE II—Regional Follow-Up Meetings

Direct-Sales Team

   • 2 days of classroom training
   • Recommended modules will cover:

       a. Establishing Credibility & Trust (Active Listening)
       b. Prospecting at High Levels
       c. Customer-Focused Sales Interviews (FIND)
       d. Customer-Focused Presentations: Crafting Unique Solutions

Channel Partner Account Manager Development

   • 2 days of classroom training
   • 35 participants
   • Recommended modules will cover:

       a. Establishing Credibility & Trust (Active Listening)
       b. Prospecting at High Levels

    c. Customer-Focused Sales Interviews (FIND)
    d. Customer-Focused Presentations: Crafting Unique Solutions
    e. Partnering With Resellers

Business Development

- 2 days of classroom sessions
- 21 participants
- Recommended modules will cover:

    a. Establishing Credibility & Trust (Active Listening)
    b. Executive Bridging/Team Selling
    c. Customer-Focused Sales Interviews (FIND)
    d. Customer-Focused Presentations: Crafting Unique Solutions

PHASE III—Self-Paced Reinforcement

- 2 modules
- Recommended modules will cover:

    a. Reinforcing Understanding Behavioral Styles
    b. Reinforcing Customer-Focused Sales Interviews

PHASE IV—Sales Management Training

- Classroom training: 2.5 days
- Recommended modules will cover:

    a. Creating a Motivational Environment
    b. Developing Your Salespeople
    c. Coaching & Counseling
    d. Setting Goals and Communicating Expectations
    e. Sales Leadership
    f. 360-Degree Feedback

PHASE V—Distance Learning: All

- Live instructor-led Internet sessions: 90 minutes each
- Sessions scheduled as needed
- Minimum of 25 participants per session
- Recommended modules will cover:

    a. Overcoming Objections
    b. Win-Win Negotiations
    c. Gaining Commitments To Action/Closing

    d. Executive Bridging/Team Selling

    e. Time & Territory Management

    f. Writing to Get Action

Research Necessary for Course Development (4 days)

- Interview the Managers to gain input and expectations.
- Spend one to two days in the field to observe skill level, sales situations and customer needs.
- Make sales calls with Account Executives and visit 2–3 customers and prospects to understand their needs and why they selected MRE.

Key Elements of Our Approach

Our professional sales approach stresses the following key elements:

- Helping people get what they want and need.
- Helping people achieve their business and personal goals.
- Customer-focused selling versus product-focused selling.
- Selling intangible value-added benefits versus product or program features
- Gaining and growing "Customers for Life"
- Doing what's right!—Doing your best!—Treating people as they'd like to be treated

Our Philosophy

We believe that all prospective customers and all subordinates have several unasked questions:

1. Can I trust you?
2. Are you committed?
3. Do you really care about me?
4. Can I depend on you?

While they may not ask these questions, they are interested in knowing the answers. If they do feel positive, the potential is there for a long-term relationship.

Some people feel it takes months or even years to establish the trust and credibility to answer these questions. We know there are specific practical actions that can be taken to accomplish this important goal quickly. This results in a happier, more productive sales team and "customers for life."

CRKInteractive Methodology to Achieve the Outcomes You Want

Our Approach—Creating the Best Program for Client

Below is the approach we will take to create the most effective program for your organization. Please note that all phases are led by *successful sales and management professionals*, with in depth knowledge of the program.

1. *Research:* The first step in creating this program is to *fully* understand your environment. We will:
   - Interview key personnel in the MRE organization, including the senior sales management VPs of the different business units to define their goals, and the business unit differences that exist and any regional differences in certain parts of the country.
   - Observe different salespeople to see what is working well, and what needs to improve. This will also allow us to understand the customer set and what they expect from MRE's sales organization.
   - Begin the "buy-in" and commitment process of the people attending the class because they are a part of its development. When they see their input reflected in the program, it enhances their involvement and commitment, which increases the effectiveness.
   - Understand the *key measurements* so that the management team can determine whether the salespeople are doing what is necessary for MRE to achieve its goals.
2. *Review:* After this research is completed, we will (if you so desire):
   - Provide a report that highlights our findings, observations and recommendations of the details for your program.
   - Begin to *"customize"* your program so that it takes the shape needed to meet your goals and objectives.
3. *Creation:* We begin to customize the program with review and input from you to make sure we are on track. Based upon start dates, we always make sure we have ample time to allocate the proper resources.
4. *Delivery:* All of your programs will be
   - Delivered by successful sales and management professionals, with in-depth knowledge, experience, and a record of success. This builds credibility and buy-in from participants, which are essential to a successful program.
   - Set up so that the number of attendees will be matched with enough resources to ensure that people get the individual attention needed.

We highly recommend the following template for delivery of MRE's "Customer-Focused Selling" program:

- Have management teams go through the key elements of Customer-Focused Selling that will be customized to meet your specific needs, based on our research and discussions. They will also make suggestions to "fine-tune" the program that will be rolled-out to their people.
- Provide the tools and coaching skills for these managers to be able to reinforce and coach their people in MRE's Customer-Focused Selling process.

5. *Follow Up and Measurement:* We will work with your management team on the most effective ways to coach, counsel, measure, and develop the program. Our 21st Century Leadership program will include specific tools to help managers reinforce and coach the Customer-Focused Selling process.

6. *Ongoing Development:* As your needs evolve, so does your program. We will work with you to adapt the program so that it meets the needs of your changing environment. We can also add to the initial programs with additional modules or elements.

CRKInteractive Core Competencies

1. Our backgrounds and experience as senior sales executives from the technology industry allow us to quickly identify our clients' most important sales priorities, along with their management and leadership needs.

2. We design customized sales and leadership development programs to address our client's needs and priorities and include top management's goals and objectives as an integral part of the program.

3. We design and deliver results-oriented training programs using the Internet, thereby maximizing productivity, saving time, and reducing expenses.

4. We deliver the development programs and coach participants on how to achieve top management's goals and objectives.

5. We design and conduct customized leadership, coaching, and team-building workshops to develop salespeople, team leaders, and sales managers along with senior management.

6. We have international and multicultural experience, which allows us to provide diverse and global solutions to our clients serving markets around the world.

7. We can conduct "train-the-trainer" sessions with complete training kits for first-line sales managers and trainers so they can lead their own training sessions.

Areas We've Helped Our Clients Address

Sales Team Related

1. Salespeople are not focused on customers' business objectives and need to use a *consultative approach* to sell additional products and services at key accounts.
2. Salespeople are too *"product-focused"* or *"technology-focused"* instead of *"customer-focused"* and are trapped into competing for *"price-based transactions"* rather than selling *"value-based solutions."*
3. Salespeople spend too much time and effort with customers who shop for a lower price rather than focusing on *customers willing to pay for value-added services*.
4. Salespeople are more comfortable interacting at lower levels of the customer's organization instead of *developing strong business relationships* at executive levels.

Sales Management Related

1. Sales managers are promoted from the ranks and have not been given the *leadership and coaching tools* to become great sales leaders.
2. Sales managers are not spending enough time *coaching and developing* their team.
3. The organization needs a common sales *process* for sales managers to implement and reinforce that creates momentum and sustains enthusiasm.

Recent Clients

- AT&T—Several Divisions
- Apple Computer, Inc. (Heath/Zenith Business Centers Sales Group)
- Applied Technologies Ventures (ATV)
- Avnet Computer
- Compaq Computer Corporation—Systems Services Division
- Computer Associates International, Inc.—Worldwide
- Dell Computer
- EMC
- Gates/Arrow Distributing
- General Electric—Distribution
- Halliburton
- JP Morgan/Chase
- Lucent Technologies
- NCR Corporation—several divisions in the USA and Internationally
- Navisite
- Okidata

- Seagate Technology
- Sunoco
- Tech Data Corporation

What Sets CRKInteractive Apart from Others?

- Our courses are customized to meet your specific needs and help you achieve immediate results.
- Our unique combinations of "blended learning" solutions minimize time out of the field and reduce costs.
- We have a record of reducing sales cycle time by as much as 30%. This allows your salespeople to generate more revenue in the same time frame, and accelerates the return on your training investment.
- Salespeople embrace our "common sense" process because it is easy to use and they experience rapid results.
- Senior sales executives with a proven track record of sales development and coaching teach our workshops.

Workshop Methodology

- Our approach is to thoroughly research your sales situation in advance by spending time in the field with your people to observe their abilities and most pressing needs.
- We will work with you to include a real-time specific sales objective to be accomplished as a result of our coaching.
- Our workshops are unique in that they feel more like an interactive sales meeting than a training session.
- Strong emphasis is placed on account bonding with the latest techniques in *relationship building* and professional selling.
- Participants compete in "real world" simulations.
- A Personal Action Plan is written by each participant detailing what, how, and when the techniques will be applied.
- A sales manager's "After the Class" monitoring and reinforcement system assists executive management in achieving their goals.

The MRE Sales Process

"Customer-Focused Selling" Course Content

Classroom

1. Behavior Styles and Selling Styles
2. Establishing Credibility & Trust/Active Listening
3. Prospecting at High Levels
4. Customer-Focused Sales Interviews—FIND
5. Customer-Focused Presentations: Crafting Unique Solutions
6. Partnering with Resellers *(Channel Account Managers)*
7. Executive Bridging/Team Selling *(Business Development Team)*

Live Instructor-Led over the Internet

1. Overcoming Objections
2. Win-Win Negotiations
3. Gaining Commitments to Action/Closing
4. Executive Bridging/Team Selling
5. Time and Territory Management
6. Writing to Get Action

Self-Paced Reinforcement

- Reinforcing Understanding Behavior Styles
- Reinforcing Customer-Focused Sales Interviews

"21st Century Leadership" Course Content

Classroom

1. Creating a Motivational Environment
2. Sales Leadership
3. Setting and Communicating Goals and Expectations
4. Developing Your Salespeople
5. Coaching and Counseling Salespeople in Customer-Focused Selling
6. 360-Degree Feedback

Self-Paced Reinforcement

- Managing Performance Discussions

Course Descriptions—Customer-Focused Selling

1. **Behavior Styles and Selling Styles**

Objective: To read another person's behavior style to deal with that person in the way he/she prefers. To become aware of your behavior style and how you affect other people.

Anticipated Outcome/Benefits: The person who can effectively read, adapt, and respond to another person will add to his/her interpersonal relations skills and grow as a salesperson and as a manager. This module will identify the different personality types salespeople encounter, and how to best interact with these people.

Overview: Every person has distinct ways of thinking, feeling, and acting, which reveal themselves in their behavior. These behaviors can be grouped into four major categories and 18 distinct styles. People who can recognize or "read" another person's behavior style are able to adjust their interaction. Armed with this knowledge, salespeople can communicate more effectively with different people.

Participants will also get to know themselves better. They will see how they actually project themselves when meeting others. They will discover the behavior traits that, in their judgment, are ideal for their career. With this information they can, if needed, make adjustments to be more successful.

Teaching Method: This module will involve a group discussion of the different behavior styles and on motivation. A short video will be viewed showing different personality traits encountered by salespeople followed by participants taking the *Personal Profile System instrument*. This instrument determines which behavior style participants demonstrate when at work. The *Personal Profile System* has been administered to over 63 million people since its development.

Participants will study their results and learn how and why they affect people in both positive and negative terms. Most importantly, participants will learn what they can do to positively motivate the people they wish to influence. The module concludes with participants viewing two other short videos to help them to adapt their interactions positively, group discussions, eight (8) people-reading exercises, and three (3) selling situation role-plays.

Module Outline

    A. Introduction
    B. Objective/Benefit Statement
    C. Overview
    D. The Four Dimensions of Behavior—Short Video
    E. Motivation Principles
    F. The Personal Profile System Instrument
    G. Understanding Your DiSC Style
    H. Behavioral Tendencies of the Four Major Styles—Short Video
    I. Work Behavior Characteristics
    J. Reading People Exercise—Short Video
    K. DiSC Behavior Characteristics
    L. Personality Expectations Exercise
    M. Motivating and Communicating Positively with the Four Behavioral Styles
    N. Using DiSC in 3 Sales Role-plays
    O. Action Plan

2. Establishing Credibility and Trust—Active Listening

Objective: To provide salespeople a specific method of how to build and maintain credibility, trust and rapport with top decision-makers and executives quickly. To practice these techniques so they become proficient with them.

Anticipated Outcome/Benefits: Participants will learn a proven method for building credibility, trust and rapport quickly with high-level decision-makers and executives. Customers prefer buying from people whom they trust and feel comfortable with. This module will teach salespeople how to build trust and rapport deliberately. It will help them shorten the sales cycle in opening new accounts.

Overview: This module will talk about what sales greats do to deliberately build trust, rapport, and confidence with their prospects and customers. Techniques from these sales greats, called "Pacing," will be studied and modeled. Participants will learn how they can control the emotional climate.

They also learn that they may be explaining about MRE too early when they meet new prospects. They will learn why it is important to ask good questions and let the prospect do most of the talking. Some people also will learn that they may actually challenge their prospects unconsciously, which damages rapport.

This module will explore these problem areas, and offer a proven method for getting on common ground to build credibility, trust, and rapport immediately (Pacing).

Teaching Method: This module begins with a group discussion of the characteristics used by superior salespeople to build credibility, trust and rapport. The facilitator will identify and model four proven techniques that sales greats use to control the emotional climate and get on common ground with prospects. The importance of listening will be discussed. Techniques to Listen Actively will be reviewed and practiced.

The class will then split into smaller groups to practice these techniques. There will be several practice sessions followed by six (6) short practice role-plays.

Module Outline

    A. Introduction
    B. Objective/Benefit Statement
    C. Overview
    D. Controlling the Emotional Climate through Pacing
    E. Four Elements of Trust
    F. Pacing Techniques to Get on Common Ground
    G. Practice Sessions for Developing Trust and Rapport
    H. The Problem of Explaining Too Much
    I. Avoiding Challenging Statements
    J. Active Listening
    K. The Personal Listening Profile
    L. 3 Practice Sessions
    M. 6 Short Role-plays
    N. Action Plan

3. Prospecting at High Levels

Objective: To show participants how to increase their penetration with high-potential accounts using a scientific method of prospecting. To teach salespeople how to prepare for each sales call in advance to create and maintain interest with top executives.

Anticipated Outcome/Benefits: This module will help salespeople increase their market share, sales volume, and income by showing them how to prospect and plan for new business and target new accounts.

The key elements of who to call, what to say to create interest, and how to gain commitments to sell deeply into an organization at multiple levels will be thoroughly examined.

Overview: To make a territory grow and become productive, high-level prospecting at strategic accounts must become a daily habit. This module will teach salespeople how to develop existing customers into "Active References."

They will understand how to leverage themselves and use the influence of their customers, business friends, and associates. They will learn how to prospect for new business within existing accounts and what to say when first approaching top-level executives at strategic accounts to create and maintain interest.

The Sales Call Planning section of this module will teach the salesperson the proper method for selling solutions. Each contact with top prospects should have an objective. Proper planning allows the salesperson to control the flow of each conversation. Instead of guessing about the prospect's interests, each salesperson will learn how to influence the flow of the conversation with a little advanced planning. This helps the salesperson talk to the right person, be relevant, avoid surprises, anticipate questions, have answers ready, save time, and sound professional.

Teaching Method: This module will involve a discussion of the types of leads and their sources. The facilitator will provide a basic overview of how to classify the importance of some leads over another. The facilitator also will show salespeople how they can upgrade their lead sources and turn present customers into active references for them. There will be an exercise to practice techniques making initial approach calls at key accounts, and exercises to practice techniques that will maintain high interest levels of top executives. We will share coaching techniques on how to improve each sales call. These are intended to show salespeople how to gain commitments to sell through additional levels within the organization.

The importance of sales call planning will be discussed. There will be a dialog with the class concerning the type of information needed by the salesperson before the sales call, and where to get this information. A Sales Call Planning format will be introduced and discussed.

An example of a sales call plan will be presented. Salespeople will complete a sales call planning exercise for one of their target accounts. As a homework assignment and reinforcement exercise, participants will complete the *Sales Action Planner* (an online sales tool) for key individuals at one of their target accounts.

Module Outline

    A. Introduction
    B. Objective/Benefit Statement
    C. Overview
    D. Lead Classification
    E. Upgrading Leads
    F. Skill Exercise—Determining Useful Customer Information and Where To Get It
    G. Skill Exercise—Creating an Initial Benefit Statement
    H. Approaching Key Accounts
    I. Warming up "Cold Calls"
    J. Sales—Call Planning by the Numbers
    K. Setting Sales Call Objectives
    L. What Is Important to My Prospect?
    M. Questions to ask
    N. Objections to Anticipate—Responses
    O. Rating My Effectiveness after the Call
    P. Homework Exercise—Sales Call Planning with the Online Sales Action Planner Tool
    Q. Action Plan

4. Customer-Focused Sales Interviews—Discovering Your Prospect's Needs and Wants

Objective: To show salespeople how to put together the various probing and questioning skills to discover the prospect's important business needs, goals, priorities and their personal win. To teach salespeople a professional interview process to move the sale forward.

Anticipated Outcome/Benefits: This module will structure competitive selling. It will show how to establish credibility, how to qualify faster, and to save time selling to a new account or increasing business at existing accounts.

Overview: Even experienced salespeople misread a prospect's or customer's interests and needs. This module will teach salespeople how to identify at least three (3) major NEEDS and WANTS before making a *Customer-Focused* sales presentation.

Organizational Dynamics, and Key Areas of Prospect Interest will be examined. The "F.I.N.D. Interview System" will be introduced and examined. F.I.N.D. stands for Facts, Important Issues, Needs, and Dreams, and is critical to conducting a Customer-Focused Interview. This module will allow salespeople to experiment with different questioning techniques to determine a prospect's dominant buying motives and their compelling reason to buy.

Teaching Method: This module will examine the differences between *Product-Focused* or *Technology-Focused* versus *Customer-Focused Selling.* The facilitator will show participants how to uncover the prospect's needs, wants, and their personal win. The first exercise will present a list of job titles that salespeople call on regularly. The class will develop the key interests important to each person.

The facilitator will then introduce the "F.I.N.D. Interview System." There will be a discussion of the most effective open- and closed-ended questions to use with this system. Salespeople will look at several examples of these questions and then add questions they would ask. Results will be shared with the entire class. The instructor will model the F.I.N.D. interview system for the group and will lead a debriefing session. Three interactive role-plays will follow.

Module Outline

- A. Introduction
- B. Objective/Benefit Statement
- C. Overview
- D. Organizational Dynamics—Areas of Interest for Different People
- E. The F.I.N.D. Interview System—Conducting an Effective Sales Interview
- F. Determining the Facts with Open/Closed Questions
- G. Identifying—Ranking—Exploring 3 Important Areas of Interest
- H. Determining Important Needs and Problem Areas
- I. Finding The Prospect's Dream (Their Personal Win)
- J. Four (4) Skill-Building Practice Sessions
- K. Tying It All Together
- L. Three (3) Interactive Role-plays
- M. Action Plan

Author's Note: I have omitted D'Innocenzo's customer-focused description of the other modules to save space. They are all similarly built around client outcomes.

Ten Key Benefits to Client for Selecting CRKInteractive

1. You will receive customized sales training from skilled instructors to meet MRE's exact requirements and address critical issues.
2. Your managers will develop and practice the practical skills needed to lead the organization to achieve MRE's objectives.
3. Your sales team will successfully shift from price-based transactions to value-based solutions.

4. Your entire sales and communications teams will better articulate the MRE value proposition to help the organization become more profitable.
5. Your sales team will learn to build stronger and longer lasting relationships with clients and prospects in order to drive continuous revenue.
6. You sales team will know how to accelerate the selling cycle with advanced prospecting, qualifying, and closing methods.
7. MRE will reduce turnover of high potential people and save a solid percentage of the expenses associated with hiring and training.
8. You will enhance your motivational and team environment for employee and company growth.
9. Your people across all levels will improve their effectiveness for listening, uncovering, and responding to customer needs with creative solutions.
10. You get our finest team. We leverage over 14 years of coaching salespeople and developing leaders to achieve the specific results you want. This is not training for the sake of training. We are *committed* to your success.

Implementation Time Frame

- Fact-Finding Research   4 days end of June
- Course Development   July 1–14
- Phase I—Kick-off Initial training   July 23
- Phase II—7 two-day Regional Sessions   August
- Phase III—Self-Paced Online   September
- Phase IV—21 Century Leadership   September
- Phase V—Live Instructor-led Internet   Ongoing

Investment Summary

1. Fact Finding Research to Customize Course Materials

   4 days @ $X,000/day $X,000

2. "Customer-Focused Selling"
   - Includes self-paced reinforcement courses
   - Includes all workbooks and materials
   - Instruction by senior facilitators

   Kickoff During July Sales Meeting $XX,000
   Regional 2-day Classroom Sessions $X00/person
   Ongoing Internet Sessions $X,000/class

   - Up to 50 participants/class
   - To be delivered as needed on an ongoing basis

3. "21st Century Leadership" $X,500/person

   • Fact-finding research to determine best practices, and set up quantitative scorecard; individualized 360 feedback report
   • Summary roll-up report
   • Interactive coaching session
   • Two and a half day management session to review the general 360 feedback results and sharpen the sales leadership and coaching skills

4. Travel Expenses Additional
5. Facilities Provided by MRE (classroom, a/v equipment)
6. Payment Terms: 1/3 due upon signing letter of agreement

   1/3 due when training starts
   1/3 due upon training completion

Investment Analysis

Assumptions

1. *Audience:* Approximately 400 Sales Representatives & Management Executives
2. *Investment:*

Fact-Finding	$XX,000
Kick-off	XX,000
Regional Classroom sessions (400 @ $X000)	XXX,000
Distance Learning Sessions (6 @ $X,000)	XX,000
Sales Leadership (45 @ $X,500)	XX,500
Total	$XXX,500

3. *R.O.I.*

Estimated incremental sales increase	5 to 10%
Previous year's revenues	$200 million
Estimated incremental sales revenue	$10 to $20 million

References

Please note: the original list contains names, titles, addresses, phone numbers, and e-mail addresses.

Testimonials

[Please note that these quotes are real. In any actual proposal the quotes are real, and the names and companies are listed in full. Mr. D'Innocenzo expects that the prospect/reader will call several of the people who are quoted. So should you. If your proposal contains testimonial quotes without real names and addresses, they will have no—or even negative—effect.]

"... Absolutely worth the investment ... Your Customer Focused Selling program was not only informative, but extremely motivational. Your pre-session research and preparation resulted in a highly effective and credible seminar. As you know, we had some of our parent company's trainers audit the class, and they were equally impressed.... my reps have truly embraced this process and it has significantly contributed to our ability to sell upon value as opposed to just price ..."

Jonathan. C.
Vice President, U.S. Sales
Company

"... Delighted with the partnership ... you began the Customer Focused Selling program for our Territory Managers.... TM's were not calling on the executive ranks of our clients. Today, without exception, executive bridging is occurring in all of our Territory Managers' focused accounts ... we implemented ... for our Inside Sales organization. Our intent of aligning the account management strategies of our inside and outside sales forces continues to be a success ... thank you for exceeding our expectations ..."

Barbara. J.
Manager of Sales Training and Development
Company

"As you know, our environment is extremely dynamic. Recent changes in our market are rapidly making the sales process more complex—we now have to call higher and on more fronts to effect sales that would have been simpler and quicker just a few months ago. The results are in and they exceeded our expectations! The feedback from the 21st Century Leadership and Customer Focused Selling training was excellent. I believe this training will help us achieve our planned growth of 150% this fiscal year and would gladly recommend CRKInteractive to any organization that is looking to increase sales productivity, qualify and close new business opportunities, and sharpen the leadership skills of the management team."

Andy S.
Vice President, Sales
Company

"Let me start by saying how unique you have been in developing and modifying programs that recognize our constantly changing needs in all areas, including sales, leadership and customer service. This is in contrast to previous vendors, and your competitors that try to pound their methodology or process into our business. Your experience as facilitators and business people has benefited us both in the specificity of the materials, as well as bringing real world experience into the actual classroom."

Sam M.
Director of Field Operations
Company

"... It was interesting to see such a high level of interaction from the group, and all of the presentations were relevant, informative and entertaining. 'These guys are fun and really know what they're talking about' was the prevailing attitude, and as you saw by the individual feedback sheets the session could only be described as a major success. The interviewing work you did prior to the session really paid off."

Dan R.
Vice President, Public Sector
Company

"XYZ International Service has progressed from a new start up organization, with no partners and no revenue, to $315 million in sales in six years. In addition we have secured partnerships with over 175 companies, such as Microsoft, Dell, Toshiba, Citibank, Marriott, and USA Today to name a few. I attribute this success, in part, to CRKInteractive's professional sales training. In addition to helping my team improve their selling skills and accelerate their sales cycles, the CRKI sales training had a rejuvenating effect on them that helped recharge their batteries and get back to basics ... it was worth the investment of time and money."

Dean C.
Vice President, Business Development
Company

Appendices

Gerry Young

APPENDIX A: FINANCIAL RATIOS

Financial ratios are used widely in banking and venture capital. They offer an easy way to measure key aspects of a company's performance and to compare them with other companies in the same industry. If you know a friendly banker, he or she might allow you to see a copy of the Robert Morris or of the Risk Management Association ratio information for companies in your line of business. Or you can find a copy in your library. If so, you can impress your potential readers by including these ratios in your analysis. *Warning: If you do this, be prepared to explain any negative variances from the industry averages, as well as any positive (favorable) variances because of results that are much larger than the industry average.*

Generally, standard ratios are divided into four categories, with each category measuring a different type of financial variable.

These categories are:

- Liquidity—Is the company able to pay its obligations when they're due?
- Activity—Is the company efficiently using its various assets?
- Capital Structure/Leverage—Does the company depend too little or too much on debt financing?
- Profitability—How profitable is the company compared to its revenue, asset or equity levels?

Table A.1 lists the common ratios by category, how they're calculated, and how they're interpreted.

APPENDIX B: ESTIMATING AND CALCULATING DIRECT COSTS

It can be difficult to know where to get started on figuring out what all the components of direct cost are for a given product, service or revenue bucket. We'll give you a few examples to make this a little clearer, but let's first set out a couple of general rules:

Table A.1
Financial Ratios

Ratios	How They're Calculated	How They're Interpreted
Liquidity Ratios		
Current Ratio	= Current Assets/Current Liabilities	This ratio should be greater than 1; the higher the better
Net Working Capital Ratio	= (Current Assets − Current Liabilities)/Total Assets	This ratio should be positive; the higher the better
Net Cash Flow as Percent of Revenue	= Net Cash Flow/Total Annual Revenue	This ratio should be positive; the higher the better
Activity Ratios		
Receivables Turnover	= Sales/Average Accounts Receivable During Period	The higher the better, to show your receivable balance isn't too high compared to your revenue.
Average Days of Receivables	= 360/Receivables Turnover	This should be low, preferably under 45 days. Old accounts receivable equal "bad" accounts receivable
Total Assets Turnover	= Sales/Average Total Assets During Period	The higher the better; this shows you're using your assets effectively
Capital Structure Ratios		
Debt/Equity Ratio	= EOY Total Liabilities/EOY Equity	These two ratios can be either too high, showing you're relying too much on debt, or too low, indicating you aren't using enough debt.
Debt/Total Assets Ratio	= EOY Total Liabilities/EOY Total Assets	
Interest Coverage Ratio	= EBIT/Interest Paid	The higher the better. A value that's too low shows the potential investor that you're skating too close to the line of not being able to meet your debt payment obligations.
Profitability Ratios		
Return on Assets	= Net Income/Average Total Assets During Period	Profitability ratios are always "the higher the better." Equity investors will look closely at the second one.
Return on Equity	= Net Income/Average Equity During Period	
Profit Margin	= Net Income/Gross Revenue	

1. *Don't worry about the small stuff.* If you're sitting there looking at a stack of invoices from the last several months, or sitting around a table with your key staff people trying to figure out this direct cost puzzle, you can start by setting aside any invoice that's so small it can't have any noticeable effect on your direct costs. Let's say your smallest monthly revenue bucket is $100,000, and you're staring at a bill for $15. This can't possibly have any noticeable impact on your direct costs as a per-cent of revenue (which is the key measure), so set it aside and move on to a more important item.

2. *Use common sense (cautiously).* Generally, especially if you're an experi-enced business manager or know a lot about the industry you're work-ing in, you can eliminate many of the invoices or vendors because you just *know* that they have absolutely no connection to the direct costs for your various revenue buckets. The problem is that sometimes common sense will lead you astray. For example, people are used to looking at telephone bills as a typical operating (fixed) expense, rather than a direct cost. In a few paragraphs below, however, we'll show how this category can become an important direct (variable) cost. So the mes-sage here is to use your common sense, but keep an open mind for items that may actually be direct cost, even though your first reaction is that they aren't. One way to double-check yourself on this is to look at the various line items that make up the total invoice cost and make sure you understand how each one is billed. When in doubt, compare an invoice to one from an earlier period when your revenue levels were much different and see what items changed and which didn't. Clearly there can be other reasons for the changes than just the varia-tion in revenue or customer levels, but this may point you to asking some of the right questions.

One of the benefits you'll get from having gone to all this work will be the ability to track margins by each revenue bucket. You should do this analysis outside your normal financial reports, by setting up report tem-plates that will capture the information each month. Your accounting soft-ware, if you use any, should be able to export information into a spreadsheet program such as Microsoft Excel.

Here's an example of how a simple report layout can be set up that will help you.

Example #1: Outside Salespeople

Many companies use some sort of outside sales force. We mentioned that you will likely have to include their commissions as part of your direct cost for some of your revenue buckets. When you dig into this area, however, you'll probably find some other costs associated with your direct sales force that should be considered direct costs. Here are a few examples to think about (there may be lots of others, depending on how you organize and run your business):

- Travel and entertainment costs for the salespeople, including mileage costs for their cars. Be careful about including the entire cost of, for example, a leased car. However, if it's used entirely or almost entirely for calling on customers, it starts looking like a direct cost.
- Cell phone or calling card expenses related to sales activities.
- Costs of collateral sales material used by the salespeople.
- Here's a potential big one: The loaded salary costs of direct support people whose job is to assist with sales-related tasks, such as researching possible contacts, collating sales leads, etc.

Example #2: Telemarketing or Inbound Call Centers

A lot of companies have an outbound call center to call prospective customers, and some have inbound call centers, where customers call to place orders, ask questions about products, and so on. You want to be careful about imputing all the staffing costs of these operations, but here are some large potential direct costs that may look at first glance like operating (fixed) costs:

- Telecommunications costs. This can be a big expense for these operations. In the case of the outbound call centers, a lot of calls have to be made to get one sale, and the telecomm costs keep mounting up for all the calls that didn't result in a buy, as well as for the successful ones.
- MARGINAL costs of adding people to the call center. This can include supervisors, trainers, and similar positions if they have to be added as part of your expansion.

Costs like these should be calculated based on the incremental cost as you add customers. For example, if your current call center staff handles $100,000 per month of business at a telecomm calling cost of $5,000 and you expect this ratio to continue, your telecomm costs would be 5 percent of revenue. Similarly, if it now takes ten people to handle a sales volume of $1,000,000, and you don't expect any noticeable efficiencies[1] to occur, you'd have to budget the loaded cost[2] (base plus incentives, payroll taxes, benefits, etc.) of one person for each $100,000 increase in revenue. If this loaded cost turned out to be $3,000 per month, you would assume that it costs you 3 percent of revenue to cover the variable costs of call center staffing.

Example #3: Website Sales

Websites can be a cost-effective way of bringing in business without hiring a lot of people and incurring the costs that go along with them (office space, computer equipment, travel expenses, and so on). They have their own cost structure, a lot of which is probably billed on a "fixed" basis. For example, you can contract with a vendor to get a website capacity that will handle a certain amount of stored data, of traffic, and so on. As your traffic grows, you'll have to keep expanding this, so your monthly costs will keep going up. This isn't a bad thing—it may still be the most efficient way to bring in new customers, but you have to expect this cost pattern.

Depending on your software and systems, you may also have to keep adding "back office" people to process the orders and questions that come in through your website. So your direct (variable) costs for this operation may include:

- Marginal costs of website expansion. You'll need to figure out a way to express this as a percent of new revenue. Ask yourself this: If my web business grows by 1,000 new sales per month, how much would my website costs go up? Then just multiply those new sales by your expected revenue per sale, and you'll know the website's expansion costs as a percent of added revenue.
- Back-office support costs. These may be high if everything has to happen manually once an order comes in from the website, or low if you've invested in systems that will automatically perform the order entry, customer setup, credit checking, etc.
- Credit card fees. Don't forget these! Almost all website sales are made using credit cards, and you'll have to pay your regular fee to the card providers. As your volume grows, you can certainly negotiate your fee level downward, but this cost will always be there.

Calculating the Cost Factors

For some types of cost that you've identified as "direct," it'd probably be best to directly determine this each month based on actual records, rather than actual cost factors. Examples of these may include:

- Cost of goods or materials purchased for resale or as input for manufacturing.
- Freight costs associated with getting material to you and to your customer.
- Sales commissions (depending on how complex your commission system is).

For most other factors, a "cost study" conducted at regular intervals will probably be sufficient. Let's take an example—telecommunications costs for your call center—and show how a cost study might be done. The result of this study will be a factor, usually expressed as a percent of revenue, that you can apply to a given situation.

Your business judgment will tell you when a single study will be good enough for all your revenue buckets, or if the differences in behavior are significant enough to make separate studies worthwhile. Let's say your buckets are "Government," "Commercial," and "Residential," indicating different types of customers. For our example (telecommunications costs in the call center), your call center people should be able to tell you whether the key calling statistics (number of calls, the time of day you get them (busy or slack periods), the average call duration, and so on) are different between these three types of customers. If it seems as though the differences might be large, go ahead and do a separate cost study for each one and compare the results. If they're close to each other, using a single figure for all the channels might be fine.

Your call center phone system should be able to capture statistics that'll tell you figures like these:

- Number of calls per day
- Average hold time per call (time spent on hold waiting for a CSR)
- Average conversation time

You'll also be able to find out your cost per minute for these calls by looking at your phone bill.[3] So let's say you found out the following regarding commercial customers:

- The current monthly revenue for the commercial segment is $300,000.
- The cost per call-minute for inbound calls to your call center is $0.0295 (taxes included).

Table A.2 shows how to calculate the telecomm cost for inbound calls to your call center as a percent of revenue.

Once you've done this model once, you don't have to re-invent it; just put in new figures and have it recalculate automatically. You should revisit each of these on a regular basis—at least twice a year—to make sure they

Table A.2
Calculation of Telecomm Cost as Percent of Revenue

Monthly Revenue (Commercial segment):	$30,000.00		Data from current financials
Cost per call-minute (inbound calls):	$0.0295		From telecomm bill or contract
Daily calls to call center from commercial customers:	437		
Average time spent on hold per call:	0.750	minutes	Data obtained from call center statistics or from specialized phone system
Average conversation time per call:	2.350	minutes	
Total billable call time per call:	**3.100**	minutes	Calculated: Total of wait time plus conversation time
Resulting total billable call time per business day:	1354.7	minutes	Calculated: Billable time per call times calls per day
Cost per business day:	$39.96		Calculated: Minutes per day times cost per minute
Business days per month:	21.5	days	Depends on holidays, etc.
Total cost per month:	$859.22		Calculated: Business days per month times cost per day
Telecomm inbound call cost as percent of revenue:	**2.86%**	**of revenue**	Calculated: Monthly cost divided by monthly revenue

remain current. A close analysis of your monthly financial results will probably give you indications that these factors may need updating.

The same type of calculation can be done for every direct cost item you've identified. For the larger ones or those which may vary significantly, it's better to use actual figures (as mentioned above for direct cost of materials, shipping, and sales commissions).

APPENDIX C: KEY FINANCIAL TERMS

Accounts Payable: A short-term liability representing amounts due, usually to suppliers of various products and services to a business.

Accounts Receivable: A short-term asset representing amounts due to the company from customers for goods or services they've received on credit terms.

Aging Schedule: A tabulation of accounts receivable or accounts payable, usually by separation into thirty-day buckets (e.g., "Current," "30–60 days," etc.).

CAPEX: An abbreviated term for "capital expenditures," representing amounts paid for assets which will be capitalized.

Cash: All physical cash possessed by the business plus amounts immediately available in demand deposit bank accounts.

Common Stock: Shares representing ownership in the business.

Compensating Balance: A minimum deposit level required in a bank account, usually as a requirement for a bank loan. The compensating balance represents funds that aren't available to the business.

Convertible Preferred Stock: Preferred stock (see below) that can be converted, under defined terms, into common stock.

Cost of Capital: The cost to the business of raising capital, including both debt and equity. Cost of capital is commonly used as the discount rate in applying time value of money calculations.

Current Assets: Assets of the business, comprising cash, savings and investment accounts, receivables, inventory, and prepaid expenses. These must either be cash or be reasonably expected to be converted into cash or cash savings within twelve months.

Current Liabilities: Liabilities due to be paid within the next twelve months. These include accounts payable, accrued wages, tax payments, and the portion of long-term debt that must be paid in that period.

EBIT: Earnings before interest and tax.

EBITDA: Earnings before interest, tax, depreciation and amortization. Also commonly referred to as "operating income."

Equity: Ownership in the company, represented by the total of accounts such as common stock, retained earnings, etc.

Exit Strategy: The means by which equity investors can convert their holdings in the company into cash. Means to do this could include selling stock, whether in a public offering or a private transaction, or being bought out by someone else.

Financial Leverage: This defines the degree to which the firm is financed by debt as opposed to equity. High leverage (a high proportion of debt) returns higher returns to the stockholders when the firm is profitable, but increases the risk to the company if it fails to meet debt payment requirements.

Fixed Assets: The capital assets of a company, such as land, buildings, equipment, etc.

Inventory: The company's stock of goods to be sold, including finished goods, and, in the case of a manufacturing firm, work in process and raw material.

Lease: A method of financing equipment that's equivalent to an extended rental agreement. Some leases provide for a bargain purchase of the equipment at the end of the lease or have other terms that make it a "capital lease," which is carried on the financial statements as an asset with corresponding short- and long-term debt. Other leases, known as "operating leases," are treated as expenses.

Liabilities: Debts that the firm owes to other entities (individuals, other businesses, government agencies, etc.). These are separated on the balance sheet into short-term (amounts to be paid within twelve months) and long-term.

Line of Credit: A borrowing arrangement with a bank in which a company may draw down funds as needed, up to an agreed-upon limit, with the bank's concurrence. A revolving line of credit, usually collateralized with accounts receivable or inventory, is a variant of the bank line of credit.

Long-Term Liabilities: Debts which must be paid, but excluding the amounts due within the next twelve months, which are carried as current liabilities.

Margin vs. Markup: Gross margin, or gross profit, is equal to sales (or revenue) minus the direct costs related to those sales. For example, if a company sells something for $100 that had direct costs of $40, the gross margin is $60, or 60 percent of revenue. **Markup**, on the other hand, starts with cost and determines what additional percent of cost should be added to result in the sales price. In our previous example, the markup on the $40 cost was $60, or 150 percent of cost.

Market Share: The percent of revenue within a defined "market" which the company has. For example, if the total "market" was $10 million and the firm being analyzed had sales of $2 million, its market share would be 20 percent. The market could be defined broadly ("U.S. sales of men's clothing") or more narrowly ("Sales of casual men's clothing in Allegheny County").

Matching Principle: A financial concept which dictates that the term of financing being used to purchase an asset should correspond to the useful life of that asset. For example, to purchase inventory, the payment terms should be measured in months rather than years. On the other hand, purchasing of heavy equipment expected to last fifteen years should be financed on a comparable term.

Net Present Value: The value of a stream of revenues and/or expenses taking into account the "time value of money" (see below).

Net Working Capital: This is equal to current assets minus current liabilities. This should be a positive number (greater than zero) to show that the business is able to pay its current obligations.

Net Worth: The value of the equity in the company. This is equal to total assets minus total liabilities.

Operating Leverage: This means the substitution of fixed costs to increase gross margins (gross profits). For example, a firm might have fixed costs of $300,000 per month and a gross profit of 25 percent, but could institute a new process which would add $100,000 per month to fixed costs but increase gross margin by 15 percent.

Preferred Stock: This is a type of equity which has a senior claim against earnings and assets than common stock, but less than debt. Preferred stock often includes dividends, and may be convertible into common stock, depending on how the preferred stock offering was structured.

Present Value: The value at present of future amounts of cash, based on discounting these amounts back to the present using the time value of money.

Retained Earnings: The portion of profits not paid out in dividends to shareholders. This is carried on the balance sheet as a cumulative amount, growing or shrinking over time with profits or losses.

SG&A (or OpEx): "Sales, General and Administrative"—the ongoing expenses of the firm other than direct costs, interest, and depreciation. These normally include payroll costs, rent, travel, insurance, communications, and other normal expenses of running the "overhead" operations of a company.

Time Value of Money: It's a basic financial principle that all money has a time value cost associated with it. This time value must be taken into account, using tables or equations, when analyzing projects or investments which will last more than a year or two. Money in the future is worth less than money now, so future revenues, expenses or investments must be "discounted" back to the present in order to have a valid comparison.

Working Capital: The current assets of the firm directly related to the company's operating cycle. This would include cash, financial investments that could be liquidated within twelve months, accounts receivable, and inventory. Note that some other current assets, such as prepaid expenses, are not included in working capital.

APPENDIX D: FINANCIAL RESOURCES
ON THE WORLD WIDE WEB

Competitive Information on Other Companies

EDGAR database maintained by the SEC (Securities and Exchange Commission), http://www.sec.gov/edgar.shtml.Select "Search for Company

Filings" and then select "Companies and Other Filers." Put in the name or SIC code of the companies you're looking for. Usually the 10-K (annual filing) and 10-Q (quarterly filings) have the financial information you'll be looking for.

http://www.census.gov/epcd/www/naicstab.htm. When you go to this link, find the general category on the left-hand side that your business fits in, click on that, and then find your exact number. For example, if you're running an insurance agency, you'd first click on "Finance and Insurance" and then scroll down until you find that "52421" is the code for an insurance agency. If you know the names of your key competitors, you might also find some good information by going to their websites. Corporate websites often have a "Press Releases" or "Investor Information" section that can contain some valuable information.

Loan Sources

Small Business Administration, an agency of the U.S. Department of Commerce, http://www.sba.gov/services/financialassistance/index.html. This site explains the types of programs they offer to help small businesses expand. You should understand that these often involve more paperwork and delay than a normal commercial loan, but for businesses, particularly those who fall into special categories targeted by the SBA (e.g., minority-owned) and who are having trouble getting sufficient financing through normal channels, this can be an invaluable resource.

Bank of America, page explaining how they offer asset-based lending, http://corp.bankofamerica.com:80/public/public.portal?_pd_page_label=products/abf/index&dcIndexCE=hm&icamefrom=www.bofa.com/businesscapital. (You can find similar pages for most substantial banks.) This is lending that would be collateralized by assets of your business such as receivables, inventory, fixed assets, real estate, etc. Pages like this will show you what banks are looking for, and can help you tailor your presentation to what they expect, making you look professional and well-prepared.

Venture Capital

Vfinance, inc., http://www.vfinance.com/. By using a search engine such as Google or other similar engines, and asking for "venture capital directories" you'll get many hits for free and fee-paid sites that will help you identify prospective venture financing sources. You should troll carefully through the listings to find something that seems to suit your needs best.

Browsing on Your Own

You can also try going to your favorite Internet search engine and just browsing for topics to see what additional insights you might gain. For example, you might browse for:

- Financial forecasting
- Cost estimation
- Bank presentations
- Angel investors (add your state or region name)

NOTES

1. Actually, in call center operations, you can usually expect higher efficiencies on a cost per call basis as you add people. This is because of an effect sometimes referred to as "queuing efficiency."

2. If each new person will need equipment, such as a computer, telephone, etc., that represent one-time costs, you'll have to convert these to monthly costs by spreading the cost out over the expected lifetime. If a $3,000 computer is expected to last four years (48 months), your monthly cost would be $62.50. This ignores the time value of money (which would increase your monthly cost), but will probably be a satisfactory approximation.

3. Be sure to include state and local taxes that apply on a per-call or per-minute basis. If you have a contract for special prices with a telecomm company, as many larger users of telecomm service due, consult the contract for rates.

Index

About the Author and Contributor

AUTHOR

K. DENNIS CHAMBERS is Founder of Chambers Communications, specializing in advertising and marketing communications, project management, and technical and business writing. He also serves as Adjunct Instructor at Endicott College, and as Lecturer at Emerson College and the University of Maryland. He is the author of *Writing to Get Action*.

CONTRIBUTOR

GERRY YOUNG holds a bachelor's degree in Chemical Engineering and an MBA in Finance. He has served as Chief Financial Officer for two U.S. companies and one European multinational company, as well as serving in other senior positions for a number of U.S. companies. His specialties are corporate planning, profitability improvement, and mergers/acquisitions.